DESIGNING with LIGHT
Residential Interiors

Wanda Jankowski

Library of Applied Design

An Imprint of

PBC INTERNATIONAL, INC. ◆ NEW YORK

Distributor to the book trade in the United States and Canada

Rizzoli International Publications Inc.
300 Park Avenue South
New York, NY 10010

Distributor to the art trade in the United States and Canada

PBC International, Inc.
One School Street
Glen Cove, NY 11542
1-800-527-2826
Fax 516-676-2738

Distributed throughout the rest of the world

ROTOVISION S.A.
9, Route Suisse
CH-1295 MIES
Switzerland

Library of Congress Cataloging-in-Publication Data

Jankowski, Wanda.
    Designing with light : residential interiors / by Wanda Jankowski.
        p.   em.
    Includes indexes.
    ISBN 0-86636-142-1
    1. Lighting, Architectural and decorative. 2. Interior
decoration. I. Title.
NK2115.5.L5J35 1991
728—dc20   91-32502
                                                CIP

CAVEAT—Information in this text is believed accurate, and
will pose no problem for the student or the casual reader.
However, the author was often constrained by information
contained in signed release forms, information that could
have been in error or not included at all. Any misinformation
(or lack of information) is the result of failure in these
attestations. The author has done whatever is possible to
insure accuracy.

For information about our audio products, write us at:
Newbridge Book Clubs, 3000 Cindel Drive, Delran, NJ 08370

Color separation, printing and binding by
Toppan Printing Co. (H.K.) Ltd. Hong Kong

Typography by
Toledo Typesetting / DPC, Inc.

Printed in Hong Kong

10 9 8 7 6 5 4 3 2 1

ACKNOWLEDGMENTS

Thanks to all the design professionals who allowed their work to be included in this book. The opportunity to do this book gave me the chance to make new acquaintances, as well as to get to know the old ones a little better. It's been a delightful experience for me, because they are all nice people, as well as top-notch professionals.

I had left the lighting field a few years ago when I went to Gralla Publications to work on a magazine called DESIGNERS' KITCHENS & BATHS, but was able to return to it when Gralla Publications bought ARCHITECTURAL LIGHTING magazine and allowed me to be the Editor of it.

There are three individuals who worked with me at ARCHITECTURAL LIGHTING who will forever have my appreciation and thanks for their dedication and hard work. Without them, I could not have found the interest to begin, or sustained the energy to complete this book. Catherine Schetting Salfino is a very talented writer and superb copyeditor whose enthusiasm about lighting helped keep me caring too, even in the worst of times. Christina Lamb Trauthwein, I predict, will also have a wonderful future in publishing because of her outstanding professionalism, and ability to make things happen using unbeatable common sense and perseverance.

Also, if Daniel Shannon, former Editorial Director at Gralla Publications, hadn't been so receptive to new ideas, and encouraging and supportive of mine, I would not have written this book. Thank you, Dan, for telling me to "make it happen."

Special kudos to Kevin Clark, PBC International's Editorial Manager, who had an altogether unenviable task—to conduct a balancing act between supporting the work on the book I was doing, and nagging me to get the rest of it done after the deadline for turning in the manuscript had already passed. Thank you, Kevin, for your patience, wisdom, unflagging optimism, and trust in my ability.

Thanks also to PBC International for their faith in me and patience. I'm proud to be the author of one of their books.

Last, but by no means least, thanks to Abe Feder for being Abe Feder. We've kept in touch all the years I've been in lighting (I'm to the age where I'll only admit that it's over a decade), and every time he calls, he gives me something—an idea for an article or editorial, insights into what lighting design is, a supportive and kind word when times are tough, and honest criticism when he thinks I need it.

Though Abe had nothing to do specifically with this book, he has influenced me and how I think about lighting a great deal, so I'd like to take this opportunity to say, "Thanks, Abe," accompanied by a great, big, affectionate hug.

—Wanda P. Jankowski

CONTENTS

INTRODUCTION   6

Chapter One
Starting from Scratch — New Homes   8

Chapter Two
Remodeling and Renovating   54

Chapter Three
One Room Wonders   172

Chapter Four
New Products   205

Chapter Five
Designers on Design   221

INDEX   238

INTRODUCTION

Residential lighting design has been an underdog for decades. Though designing the lighting systems for a home can take as long as designing the lighting for an office or retail space, the fees paid to consultants were far lower. And so many fine designers were reluctant to take on residential projects because it didn't help them pay their bills.

Residential lighting design does have its own rewards, however. It offers the opportunity to get to know the clients intimately, and to tailor an element of design to their personalities and lifestyles. To know and see that the design directly affects how much comfort and enjoyment people draw into their lives daily can be very satisfying.

Times are changing. Residential lighting design is becoming more popular and widespread for several reasons. First, the field of lighting itself is maturing and becoming widely recognized as a complex and legitimate design profession. Second, people are spending less time going out, and more time retreating into the sanctuary of their homes. Spending more time at home translates into an increased need for flexibility of scene and mood. More sophisticated, layered lighting systems are a logical component in creating variety in the environment. Third, the development of more refined products has made lighting system options more affordable and feasible in the home.

This book reflects those recent developments in residential lighting design. Assembled here are examples of how residential lighting design challenges are met in conjunction with the development of interior design and architectural concepts, both in new construction and in renovations. This compiling of the lighting designs not only of practicing lighting consultants, but of interior designers and architects, is intended to provide the reader with a range of perspectives and points of view. An effort has been made to showcase diverse ideas and techniques by including projects built with different budget limitations, from different parts of the country, and with clients whose lifestyles run the gamut.

Since in the past, the clients' budget limitations often had been a major stumbling block to the hiring of lighting designers, a chapter on "One Room Wonders" has been included that reflects the growing trend among lighting consultants to restructure their fees on a room by room basis. Today, lighting design is not just for the rich and famous, but affordable to the middle class homeowner as well. A one-room remodel can cost under $1,000.

Options is a key word in describing the benefits of residential lighting today, and more options are available to today's homeowner because of advancements in product technology. Though in years past, ceiling recessed lighting was considered the forte of the residential designer, today "layering light" using a variety of fixture types and sources, is predominantly thought to produce the most flexible and effective designs. A product chapter has been included that presents a sampling of different kinds of light sources, fixture types and accessories recently introduced.

Though this book deals mainly with interiors, some exterior lighting projects have been included, because the interest in and number of residential outdoor and landscape projects is on the rise—particularly in parts of the country that enjoy a warm climate year round. The development of smaller outdoor fixtures allows equipment to be concealed in a natural setting so the lighting effects can be appreciated without the visual intrusion of the hardware.

Since residential design so closely involves exploring the behavior and psychology of the individual, it was a logical step to round out this book by adding a chapter revolving around the professionals who designed the lighting for the projects shown. The "Designers on Design" chapter is filled with practitioners' opinions on what's happening in residential lighting today, what effects energy issues might have on design in the future, what light sources will gain more widespread use in the home, tips on techniques that work, and more.

I hope you'll use Designing With Light—Residential Interiors as a source for inspiration and interesting ideas.

Wanda P. Jankowski

Chapter One

Starting from Scratch — New Homes

As families grow, or become more prosperous, even though they may opt to add on a room or rooms, rather than buy a larger house and relocate. Included here are two examples of new additions—one interior and one exterior. Even though the multi-roomed gallery was an added new space, it had to be designed to blend in with the character of the rest of the house and yet fulfill the specific requirements of the owners. The multi-part gallery houses an ever-changing art collection and is appropriate for entertaining as well. What makes this gallery different from most is the custom-designed linear baffle system that conceals the track PAR fixtures.

Poolside pavilions—two enclosed and one open-air structure—were created for clients who spend a lot of time outdoors dining and entertaining. Not only did the pavilions make their outdoor lives more enjoyable, but they lent increased visual appeal and interest to the plain-Jane boxy house. A pyramid-shaped roof is carried through and unifies all three structures. Efficient fluorescent lighting is unobtrusively integrated into the beams of the open-air and largest structure.

Though getting repeat clients is commonplace, one Palm Springs designer explores how the changes and growth in the personalities of the clients is reflected in how his designs for their residences had to grow and develop in turn. Two residences—one house, and one condominium—were designed for the same clients five years apart. The first residence is replete with neutral-toned furnishings and relies on the lighting to add subtle interest. The condominium, however, is filled with less restrained and more avant-garde lighting effects that echo the bright splashes of color, and glossy reflective materials used throughout the interior spaces.

Another residence in Palm Springs— "the land where nothing's crazy"—was designed specifically to be sold to a typical inhabitant of the area. The lighting effects installed are appropriately outrageous and clever—like the butane-gas-generated flames behind a horse's head that overlooks a swirling whirlpool bathed in blue and lavender light, and the bar area's thousand points of light that gyrate to the music of the stereo.

Many high-end clients display rare and expensive artworks in their homes. The goal for the lighting consultant is to enhance the beauty of the art, while maintaining the comfort and liveability of the residential spaces. A very liveable home filled with art objects is featured here. Concealed spotlights highlight sculptures displayed along a gallery corridor while ambient illumination is delivered in an out-of-the-ordinary fashion by custom-designed "unsconces" that look like lit dents in the walls.

DESIGNING TO SELL

The thousand miniature pilot lights in the bar can pulsate in time to music from the sound system. The glowing edge of the circular opening in the wall is not reflection, but illumination from recessed incandescent tubes.

The land where nothing's crazy, that's at the center of the entertainment business, and home base for international designers" is how James Callahan describes Palm Springs— the location of the home Callahan inhabits, but that he designed specifically to sell. That Callahan expects prospective clients to be as emotion-packed, daring, and fast-paced as the locale is evident by the inventive, no-holds-barred interior and lighting design of the residence.

Bands of red and blue neon, and color washes from filtered recessed ceiling fixtures are incorporated into the sound system that greets the visitor's eyes in the entry, and that sets the tone for the rest of the home.

In the living room, light is used as decoration: swirling circles of white light are cast on the ceiling from custom glass table lamps. Light is used as form-giver: pink 18-inch incandescent tubes are recessed around the fireplace, behind the wall unit, above pictures, and under assorted furnishings. Light is used as mood-maker: ceiling recessed MR 16

PROJECT LOCATION
Palm Springs, California
ARCHITECT, INTERIOR AND
LIGHTING DESIGNER
James Callahan, James Callahan—
A Design Corporation
ELECTRICAL CONTRACTOR
McClellan Electric
PHOTOGRAPHER
Sheldon Lettich
LIGHTING MANUFACTURERS
General Electric Co., Capri Lighting, Lumiline,
Roxter, Nova, Lutron Electronics Co. Inc.,
Custom Neon by Charles Debora, Custom
Dining Room Sconces and Bar Pilot Lights by
James Callahan

Sofas in the dining area are underlit. Custom black rectangular sconces adorn the wall on either side of the circular opening.

spotlights grazing grey suede sofas, and emphasizing the sleek smoothness of black lacquered coffee tables and flawless porcelain vases invite a feeling of romance and sensuousness.

In the bar area, light is just plain fun. A thousand miniature pilot lights can pulsate to the music at the flip of a switch, or be dimmed and subdued to act as nightlights. The perimeter of the circular opening in the wall behind the bar is lit with linear incandescents behind plexiglass.

The dining room continues the play of contrasting colors that is repeated throughout the house: dark browns and black juxtaposed against beiges and light greys. Recessed MR 16 spotlights illuminate the eating area, and rectangular black wall sconces provide a bit of drama.

Food for dining is prepared in a kitchen designed as much for socializing and entertaining as for food preparation.

"My goal is to create kitchens that don't look like kitchens, so guests can kind of filter into the kitchen so the cook can become part of the party, instead of being off alone to do the mundane and ordinary chores," Callahan says. The cabinet interiors light when the doors are opened. All the pantries are concealed behind smooth paneled doors.

In the bedroom, recessed downlights provide general illumination. Attention is drawn at night to the terrace beyond the glass sliding doors, where potted plants are grazed from below. The plants sit on plexiglass panels which are underlit by fluorescent tubes recessed in the wall.

Also outside the bedroom is a Jacuzzi—but not an ordinary Jacuzzi. This one is illuminated by 75-watt color-filtered outdoor floodlights placed at the base of the tub. But that's not all. Steam rises through small valves, "like a capuccino machine," says Callahan, and produces a magenta and purple fog. As the piece de resistance, flames from a butane torch shoot out of the top of the Grecian styled horse's head sculpture that rises above the edge of the tub.

The swimming pool beyond is illuminated at night by fiber optics recessed around its perimeter. Any takers?

Swirling patterns of light on the ceiling come from table lamps that project light upwards through clear glass bowls.

In the living room, linear incandescents float the platform and wall surrounding the fireplace.

The Jacuzzi and swimming pool are outside the sitting area in the bedroom. Uplighting of plants creates dappled patterns on the ceiling.

Callahan designed the Jacuzzi to be like a "capuccino machine" with lots of steam made especially dramatic with magenta and purple color washes.

That's a real flame shooting out of the horse's head, produced with a butane torch.

Here's a kitchen designed for socializing — comfortable stools and provisions well concealed in pantries.

Uplit plantings and recessed spotlights create a dramatic mood, unusual for a kitchen. By the way, the floor is covered with rubber tile—nothing breaks!

The sound system near the home's entrance is encased in stainless steel. Touch latch drawers hold records and compact discs.

Color washes from ceiling recessed fixtures fitted with filters intensify the effect of the red and blue neon.

"The whole concept behind the house," says lighting designer Julia Rezek, "was to bring the outdoors inside. The house had a garden-like setting wrapped around it, with pools, rippling ponds and extensive landscaping. At the entrance you can look through the living room to the outdoors beyond with the fountain out there. By lighting up the fountain, the eye is drawn through and creates the feeling that the outdoors has come inside as well."

Exterior plantings are illuminated with a variety of fixtures, including PAR 64 narrow beam fixtures that are mounted on the vertical portion of the second story.

Inside, in the large, glass-walled living room, the ceiling-recessed downlights help to focus attention on and define the seating areas. A cove lamped with staggered fluorescents provides the clients with the option of giving the ceiling a higher light level when needed.

The children's wing is marked by runs of pink neon that begin at the balcony level of the living room atrium. "This neon, when seen from the exterior through the glass block, appears as a soft pink glow—a nice effect at night"says Rezek.

"In the kitchen, the client wanted a lot of light, so we gave it to her," says Rezek. This is accomplished with recessed downlights, and fluorescent runs above and below the overhead cabinets.

View looking into the courtyard. Some fixtures are mounted on the house, others are ground mounted.

The lighting designer was called into this project at a later stage. "In fact, thousands of cans were in the ceiling everywhere," says Rezek. The existing downlights were adapted to the new lighting design by retrofitting with low-voltage units, or by complete replacement with other units.

The kitchen is illuminated with fluorescent tubes, staggered to avoid socket shadow.

The living room is enhanced by
pink neon and small aperture
recessed downlights fitted with
PAR 38 lamps.

Plays of light and shadow lead
guests down the pathway to
the main entrance.

PROJECT LOCATION
Los Angeles, California
LIGHTING DESIGNER
Julia Rezek and Ray Grenald, Grenald
Associates Ltd
ARCHITECT, LAND PLANNER, INTERIOR
SPACE DESIGNER
Barry A. Berkus, AIA
LANDSCAPE ARCHITECT
Peridian Group
PHOTOGRAPHER
Rob Miller
LIGHTING MANUFACTURERS
Halo, Lightolier, Amerlux, Lithonia, Prudential,
Alkco, McPhilben, Staff Lighting, New
Horizons, Litelab, Lutron Electronics Co. Inc.,
Nightscaping, Hydrel, Keene, Bronzelite, and
Kim Lighting

MULTI-ROOMED GALLERY

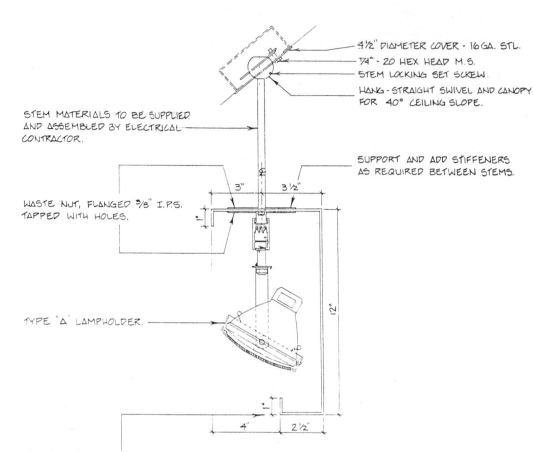

4½" DIAMETER COVER - 16 GA. STL.

¼" - 20 HEX HEAD M.S.

STEM LOCKING SET SCREW.

HANG - STRAIGHT SWIVEL AND CANOPY FOR 40° CEILING SLOPE.

STEM MATERIALS TO BE SUPPLIED AND ASSEMBLED BY ELECTRICAL CONTRACTOR.

SUPPORT AND ADD STIFFENERS AS REQUIRED BETWEEN STEMS.

WASTE NUT, FLANGED ⅜" I.P.S. TAPPED WITH HOLES.

TYPE 'A' LAMPHOLDER.

3"   3½"

12"

4"   2½"

BOTTOM EDGE OF BAFFLE TO BE LEVEL WITH TOP OF WALL IN ALL ROOMS. ADJUST STEM LENGTHS ACCORDINGLY.

L ighting designer Corinne Strumpf has incorporated museum lighting concepts into the three-part gallery addition of a New Jersey home. The clients wanted not only a flexible system that would showcase their extensive and changing art collection, but enough general illumination to accommodate entertaining guests in the spaces.

The three parts of the gallery are: the entry gallery, an upper seating area, and a lower hexagonal living room with cupola ceiling.

The custom-designed system Strumpf developed is based on a pendant-mounted baffle with a two-circuit track that provides lighting for the artworks. Low-voltage, 50-watt PAR 36 lamps are used to highlight individual details in the paintings. The 120-watt PAR 38 fixtures with spread lenses are used to wall wash.

The concealment of the lamps behind the sleek linear baffle prevents direct glare from reaching viewers' eyes, and blends in with the architecture of the space. The track circuits are divided into multiple zones via a centralized dimming system so different levels of illumination are readily available to complement changing works of art.

PROJECT LOCATION
Ringwood, New Jersey
LIGHTING DESIGNER
Corinne Strumpf, IALD, Corinne Strumpf Lighting Design
ARCHITECT
James Timpson
PHOTOGRAPHER
Frank Ritter
LIGHTING MANUFACTURERS
Edison Price, Lightolier Inc., Norbert Belfer, and Electro Controls

Downlights are angled to accommodate the sloped cupola ceiling in the hexagonal living room.

For general illumination, recessed 100-watt A-19 downlights are angled for the 40 degree slope of the main living room's ceiling. The cupola in the living room has uplight from low-voltage 3.75 strip lights. In the entry gallery, T 6.5 lamps are recessed in the sides of niches and hidden from view.

The flexibility of the system comes from the capability to change lamp types as needed. Strumpf says, "If the clients no longer want the incandescent look with its lower color temperature, next year they can change the lamps to quartz wall washers with MR 16 accent lighting, which will raise the color temperature and give the rooms a crisper look."

The designer had to include general illumination because the three-part gallery addition is used for entertaining as well as viewing of art pieces. This is the upper seating area.

The baffled pendant system allows the client the opportunity to change light levels and lamp types to complement changing works of art. Here in the entry gallery, niches are lighted at the entrance with strip lights.

DOMES IN DALLAS

The domed, skylit foyer of this Dallas penthouse is designed to make guests feel as though they've "entered a lamp" and are surrounded by a luminous glow. A small portion of the owner's extensive art collection is displayed in foyer niches that are internally lit with 20-watt AR 48 reflector lamps. The lamps come two to a strip and are concealed on the top and sides of the niches.

The skylight is illuminated at night by a circle of 3.75-watt strip lights fitted with medium-blue silicone filters and concealed in its perimeter.

"We chose medium-blue filters to create the effect of moonlight shining through the glass," says Tully Weiss, who designed the illumination for the entrance foyer, as well as the lighting control system for the entire apartment.

In addition, beams are cast on the patterned wood floor by four 25-watt, PAR 36 pinlight spots with anti-dazzle shields. They are evenly placed around the skylight's perimeter.

In addition to the custom chandelier, pinlights cast light onto the object on the tabletop.

PROJECT LOCATION
Dallas, Texas
ARCHITECT
Bill Booziotis, Booziotis & Company Architects
LIGHTING DESIGNER
Tully Weiss, Tully Weiss Lighting Design designed the foyer lighting; Bill Booziotis, Booziotis & Company, designed all other rooms
INTERIOR DESIGNER
Jerry Oden
PHOTOGRAPHER
R. Greg Hursley, R. Greg Hursley, Inc.
LIGHTING MANUFACTURERS
Lightolier, Alesco, Lite Cycle, Lucifer, and Lutron

In line with the pinspots are four circular coves in the dome that will eventually serve as canvasses for murals. In the meantime, 3.75-watt strip lights evenly illuminate the bare surfaces of these recessed ceiling cavities and add to the open feel of the space.

Two rows of strip lights concealed in the rim at the base of the dome uplight the vault itself.

In the living and dining rooms, paintings and sculpture are highlighted with wall washers and open reflector downlights fitted with 150-watt PAR 38 lamps. Ceiling coves above the marble fireplace and shuttered windows house the same lamps in adjustable spot fixtures mounted on tracks.

The downlight gives the projecting wall above the fireplace depth and dimension. Decorative candelabra sconces have been placed on either side of the fireplace.

In the dining room, a cast iron and crystal, custom-made chandelier with 12 15-watt flame-shaped bulbs in half-inch bases is suspended above the table. The crystals sparkle when hit by the light from two adjustable pinlights. The pinlights also cast illumination down onto flowers or other items placed on the table.

A second, multi-faceted dome in the woman's windowless bath above the tub is lit softly with indirect

Paintings and sculptures are highlighted with wall washers and downlights.

uplight from 24-volt strip lights with reflectors. At the vanity, 150-watt PAR 38 open reflector downlights provide illumination for grooming.

"In the kitchen, we wanted shades and shadows," says Bill Booziotis, the architect for the apartment, who also designed the lighting for all the rooms except the foyer. "It's more interesting to have layers of lighting."

Open reflector 100-watt A 19 downlights are used, as well as 150-watt PAR 38 wall-washers and 50-watt adjustable accent lights. For convenience and safety, even illumination is furnished over food preparation areas.

The domed, circular foyer is made to glow so guests can feel like they are "inside a lamp." Light surrounds the guest from the dome above and from side niches

The perimeter of the skylight has striplights concealed around it. In addition, four pinspots cast illumination upon the patterned wood floor below.

Niches are top and sidelighted with 20-watt AR 48 reflector lamps.

Even illumination is used over
the food preparation areas.

GROWING WITH THE CLIENT

Those designers who are fortunate enough to have ongoing clientele are afforded not only the opportunity of seeing the clients grow through the years, but of being able to reflect and express those personality and lifestyle changes through design.

Here are two residences designed by James Callahan for the same client—five years apart.

The clients, conservative and active in the political arena, needed a home that was suitable for the upscale entertaining of friends and business contacts. The first residence designed by Callahan was a home in Edina, Minneapolis.

Its grand scale was dictated by the extraordinarily high ceilings—15 feet. In the living and dining area, the designer used the lighting fixture arrangements to create pleasing patterns in the ceiling that mimicked circular motifs in the furnishings below.

"I normally do not like to draw attention to the ceiling," Callahan explains, "but because of the tremendous height of that ceiling, anyone walking in at that lower level before ascending the steps up to the living room was forced to look up. So we created some interesting patterns on the ceiling with the fixtures and reflections of light—circles around circles.

The Condominium: "Look at the clarity of the reflections in the ceiling," says James Callahan. "Now look down into the floor and see that wonderful ambiguous blur of color and suggestion of shape and light. All that would have been missed if I had specified a flat matte, rather than a reflective ceiling."

PROJECT LOCATION
The House, Edina, Minnesota; .
The Condominium, Minneapolis, Minnesota
INTERIOR AND LIGHTING DESIGNER
James Callahan, James Callahan—
A Design Corporation
ELECTRICAL CONTRACTOR
Sonny Miller Construction Co.
PHOTOGRAPHER
Sheldon Lettich
LIGHTING MANUFACTURERS
The House—Staff Lighting; The
Condominium—Capri Lighting, A I

The Condominium: The dining
room opens into the living
room. The mirror wall to the left
is the flip side of the split marble
wall shown in the entry.

"I get criticized for doing that especially by my architect friends. They think there's this grid pattern that they need to follow in ceilings, but what I like about the new fixtures being developed today is that they free us from being dependent upon some kind of a grid pattern," Callahan says.

The steps up to the living room are underlit with linear incandescents. The circular pattern of fixtures complements the globe-like sculpture on its cylindrical pedestal below. A circular fixture arrangement is used over the round table surrounded by chairs near the fireplace.

The rest of the ceiling has downlights only where they are needed. For example, to graze the walls around and provide general illumination in the seating area.

Linear incandescents accentuate the stepped brushed brass laminated panels around the fireplace, and enliven the recessed art niche adjacent to the fireplace.

The colors in this home are conservative—beige and navy blue. The lighting serves as a dynamic element against this neutral palette.

"Now compare that to what I designed for those clients five years later. They had a new lifestyle, and it was an interesting transition," Callahan says.

The second residence, unlike the first, was located in a 17th floor condominium in downtown Minneapolis.

"The client needed a showplace and an impressive background for social functions that would be open, airy, and dramatic," Callahan says.

The entry of this residence is filled with color and reflective materials—very different from the beiges and soft furnishings of the first home.

"Imagine you're in a red brick building in Minneapolis, walking down a Jacobean wall-papered hallway with shaggy carpeting, and the door opens, and you look into this entry space. It was the talk of the building," Callahan says.

The clients had been used to the high 15-foot ceilings in their previous home. Unfortunately, the condo didn't afford them the luxury of height. But to rescue his clients from feeling "closed in" Callahan rerouted the wiring and ductwork around the room instead of across it.

"If you look closely at the photograph, you'll see a soffit around the room. I ran everything in the ceiling—the lighting, air conditioning, and heating—around the outside, which gained me an extra 24 inches of space," Callahan says.

"The 'light box' in the entry is composed of 8-inch diameter steel tubes mounted into the black glass ceiling recess. I slit the top of the tubes open and added a rainbow effect of neon in a color spectrum inside the tubes. So you really don't see the neon as you stand underneath it. What you see is the reflection of it in the black glass of the ceiling above," Callahan explains.

The Condominium: A rainbow of neon has been inserted into the metal tubes in the ceiling soffit. The wall has a diagonal slit and lighting recessed in the edge of the lower half.

"The whole condominium only had about three walls in it. One of my goals was not to have the spaces enclosed anywhere, but to create dividers that would promote privacy, but give the clients varied stages in which to interact with guests," Callahan says.

His solution to enclosing and yet not enclosing the space was a monumental marble wall, slit diagonally into two pieces.

"I thought in terms of stalactites and stalagmites, and wondered one day, 'Why do walls have to always come down from the ceiling to the floor?'. Why can't they come from the floor and go up toward the ceiling, and from the ceiling to the floor, and why do they have to meet? This was my way of dividing off several rooms without actually confining or restricting the flow of light, air or design," Callahan says.

The underside of the top half of the wall is finished with stainless steel; the bottom has a linear source that projects a natural daylight type of illumination recessed in the edge. The linear light bounces off the stainless steel and reflects down onto the polished marble floor so guests can see how it is done.

On the other side of the wall is the dining room. The dining room side of the wall is mirrored, so guests would not be aware that it was the same room. Over the dining table are pendant fixtures made of stainless steel encircled by single rows of blue neon.

The use of reflective materials continues into the living room in floor and ceiling treatments.

"I think reflective materials extend architecture. Many times designers are forced to deal with a lot of wall coverings, carpeting, upholstery and window treatments that tend to obscure or draw attention away from the architecture. Since I used leather on the sofas and matte finishes on the cement walls, I felt I had to pick up the titillating effect of the floor reflecting back up into the ceiling," Callahan says. This was also another way to create the illusion of height in the ceiling.

The linear vertical lamps placed on the marble cube end table have been custom designed by Callahan. The two square artworks over the sofa mimic the two square windows on the adjacent wall and create an interesting synergism. Downlights with MR 16s provide ambient illumination.

Unusual is the extensive use of Corian in the dressing and bath areas. The linen closets and cabinets, bath vanities, walls and underlit bathtub are all made of Corian.

Lighting throughout the home can be set at varied levels via the dimming system.

The First House: Note the circular arrangement of downlights over the sculpture. James Callahan dared to "break the grid."

The First House: The linear
lighting accentuates the layered
panels of the fireplace and adds
life to the neutral beiges of the
interiors.

The Condominium: The corridor leading to the master suite includes a retractable fixture that illuminates the three-dimensional black artwork.

The Condominium: The drawers and closets that line the corridor of the dressing area/bath are made of Corian, as is the under-lit tub seen at the end of the corridor. Blue neon has been re-cessed into the underside of the top cabinets.

POOLSIDE PAVILIONS

This Glendale home was "kind of a plain Jane box," according to landscape architect Larry Tison. The owners wanted to take advantage of the mild California climate and enjoy poolside evenings outdoors, and yet maintain a sense of privacy from neighboring hillside homes from which their pool area could be viewed.

Tison designed three stylistically unified structures to accommodate the owners' needs. The enclosed, windowless bathhouse contains a shower, toilet, sink and changing area. The second, a glass-walled pavilion, houses a whirlpool. Each of these has a pyramid-shaped roof fitted with tiles that match those on the house, and topped with a plexiglass 4 foot by 4 foot skylight.

The third and largest pavilion in the L-shaped arrangement is an open air cedar structure that stands over the dining and entertaining area. The cedar is stained desert grey to match the trim of the house and fluorescent lighting has been incorporated into it.

Three pavilions have been built to allow the owners to enjoy the California evenings outdoors. The patio pavilion is an open air structure. The structures containing the whirlpool and bathhouse are enclosed.

PROJECT LOCATION
Glendale, California
LANDSCAPE ARCHITECT AND LIGHTING DESIGNER
Larry Tison & Associates
PHOTOGRAPHER
Christopher Covey, Christopher Covey Photography
LIGHTING MANUFACTURER
Nightscape

"We sandwiched the fluorescent lamps between the structural members and added diffusers underneath them, so you see a nice soft light and you don't see a fixture of any kind," Tison says. The fluorescent corridor is all on one switch because, Tison says, "if you're going to be out there, you're going to need all the illumination you can get."

The wrought iron railing shown in the photographs has since been dismantled and placed in storage. The railing had been installed as a safety measure because the owners' children had not yet learned to swim.

"They wanted to keep the children out of the water, but still have room for them to play," Tison says.

There is also a 4 foot by 12 foot food preparation/barbecue counter at the side of the 20 foot by 40 foot pool opposite the pavilions that is fitted with localized lighting.

The recessed fluorescent fixtures were chosen for their unobtrusiveness. The wrought iron railings have since been taken away.

The roof of the patio pavilion is slatted and does not contain glass. The cedar has been stained desert grey to match the house trim.

The structure over the patio area has been added to the house and is illuminated with fluorescent fixtures recessed into the cedar beams.

ARCHITECTURAL ARCADE

One of the striking features of this Hollywood home is an arcade filled with artwork and enhanced lighting designed by Chip Israel, Grenald Associates Ltd. "We wanted to achieve a gallery effect and also to make it a very liveable space at the same time," says Israel. In the gallery corridor, MR 16 spotlights concealed up in the soffits and connected to a multi-scene preset system accent the artwork. A softer, indirect light comes from the 'unsconces,' lamped with a tungsten source, that look like vertical light dents in the walls.

"The sconces are custom made," says Israel. "The idea was to have the light emitted from the column iteslf without applying something to the outside of the column.

At one end of the corridor, a large sculpture stands outside two glass doors. It is illuminated with waterproof MR 16 fixtures surface-mounted on the backs of beams. "The clients can dim the lights on the exterior sculpture to allow the eye to go out to the skyline beyond, or they can put the light on the sculpture, which tends to stop the eye and define the surrounding space," Israel explains.

Recessed line-voltage incandescent wall-washers are used to accent the large-scale, wall-hung art pieces.

PROJECT LOCATION
Los Angeles, California
LIGHTING DESIGNER AND PHOTOGRAPHER
Chip Israel, Grenald Associates Ltd.
ARCHITECT
Edward Fields and David Richards, Fields & Silverman
LIGHTING MANUFACTURERS
Lightolier, Prescolite

The sculptural art forms are highlighted with MR 16 recessed units.

Living room lighting is task-oriented, used to highlight art-work and provide comfortable illumination for seating areas.

Lighting in the living room had to highlight the large-scale artworks hung around the perimeter of the room, provide comfortable lighting for the individual seating areas, and furnish accent lighting for small objects and coffeetables. The lighting system designed uses recessed fixtures lamped with a variety of sources. Line voltage incandescent lamps wall wash, incandescent PAR lamps cast light down from the 12-foot ceiling to define the seating areas, and adjustable MR 16s highlight sculptural art forms.

Another example of the "lighting of tasks within a space rather than the space itself" approach is the illumination provided at the piano. "Accent light is aimed over the shoulder of the pianist so he can see the keys and read the music," Israel says. And there's another accent that highlights the top of the piano if something's displayed on it when it's closed, or if the piano is opened, the strings and soundboard inside are lighted and reflected on the black lacquer lid."

"Residential lighting is fun when we have good architecture and good art to illuminate," Israel says. "We can't do a whole lot without a good base."

GLASS HOUSE

The home's structure is composed of four concrete sections that are formed by the intersecting skylights.

Hammock Oaks, a high-end residential community in southeast Coral Gables, includes a lake with access to Biscayne Bay and the ocean beyond. The 5,000 square foot home built in a three-quarter acre lot on the lake overlooks land across the lake that is replete with mangroves, part of a national park, and an active natural game preserve.

The challenge for architect and designer Miguel Rodrigo-Mazure was to fulfill the needs of the clients—a working couple, both medical doctors, with two children—and bring to the project his own unique sense of style and perspective not only in the architecture and lighting design, but in the design of furnishings as well.

Function is served and changing moods are created by low-voltage accent lights and downlights on dimmers.

Rodrigo-Mazure has used light to define architectural spaces, as well as to take advantage of the site's natural beauty. Major components of the home's architecture are the criss-crossed skylights and large expanses of glass windows and doors, which allow sunlight to flood the open spaces within.

"The skylights deliver a very soft light," says Rodrigo-Mazure. "The top layer of glass is the reflecting glass, so the sunlight penetration is well controlled to prevent glare. The light from windows and skylights allows house inhabitants to experience the ever-changing sun and cloud conditions outside indoors."

The interior and exterior electric illumination had to achieve several goals.

"Number one was to emphasize the prominent architectural elements on the outside as well as inside," says Rodrigo-Mazure. "We used halogen lamps inside along the skylight constructions, so when you view the house from the outside, you see the light coming through the glass, illumuniating both skylights."

Fixtures have also been chosen and placed to furnish functional lighting. The tops of the low-profile bollards used outside at the entrance, driveway, and back of the house resemble fixtures also used in the pier at the dock. Inside the house, a combination of track fixtures, and recessed downlights and accent units are used to light circulation areas, and provide general ambient illumination, as well as to highlight paintings, sculpture, and decorative elements like plantings.

Large expanses of glass doors and windows maintain a visual connection to the outdoors.

PROJECT LOCATION
Coral Gables, Florida
ARCHITECT, INTERIOR AND
LIGHTING DESIGNER
Miguel Rodrigo-Mazure,
Rodrigo-Mazure Architects
ELECTRICAL CONTRACTOR
E.P.J. Electrical Contractor
GENERAL CONTRACTOR
Charlie Young
WINDOW & SKYLIGHT CONSTRUCTION
Crystal Front
STEEL CONSTRUCTION
Fagundo & Co.
PHOTOGRAPHER
Thomas Delbeck
LIGHTING MANUFACTURERS
Lightolier, Prescolite, Devine Design

Daylight from skylights is soft and ever-changing from the interaction of the clouds and sun.

Track fixtures highlight artwork, and glassblock partitions allow daylight to filter through the house.

The home's main structural components are four reinforced concrete sections that correspond to the spaces intersected by the skylight. The second floor is made of steel columns embedded in the main concrete beams. It hangs from these columns to allow the ground floor to be free of vertical supports so a free flow of space can be enjoyed. Mazure's architecture embodies a philosophy about our need for protected yet open and unimpeded space.

A catwalk that connects the upper master bedroom, the two children's bedrooms, and the loft is made of steel sections with a perforated stainless steel floor and stainless steel cables. The catwalk is connected to the concrete structure by means of steel angles, allowing the catwalk to flow freely in the main socializing area.

Rodrigo-Mazure also designed many of the furnishings and built-ins.

The catwalk is made of steel sections. It connects the bedrooms and loft area. Downlights provide circulation lighting.

Chapter Two
Remodeling and Renovating

Renovations can present designers with a myriad of problems and limitations that differ in type and degree from those presented in a new construction project. Included here are a few of the lighting design challenges renovations can present, and varied ways in which lighting design for them can be approached.

Ideally, the lighting designer should be called in at the same time as the architect and interior designer—in the early stages of design planning for a renovation. Unfortunately, in this imperfect world, circumstances can result in attention to the lighting design being left to the latter design stages of a project. Included here are some projects in which the lighting consultants had to cope the best they could with preexisting situations involving either physical limitations in the space, or partially designed spaces in which the lighting consultant was called in after the conceptual stage of the project.

A finished space in Texas was relit with adjustable, custom-designed fixtures that had to be placed in the holes formerly occupied by downlights because the ceiling finish could not be touched. Existing downlights in a California home have been either relamped or replaced with lighting that suited the tasks at hand. In a Georgetown basement apartment, 32 fixtures were used as wall sconces and to uplight barrel vaults in order to make the basement, which did not get much natural light, seem like a bright and fully windowed space.

Of course, client taste always influences a residential project, and designs have to be created based on requirements and lifestyle needs placed upon the project by the client. For example, one client in California wanted a quality of very white light in her home. This led to the designer's specification of metal halide and halogen sources, and the creation of some interesting plays of light quality when the 'white' sources were juxtaposed in some spaces with warmer cold cathode runs.

The clients in a Texas residence wanted the stunning antiques they owned showcased, and this led to the adoption of a dramatic, light-and-dark, "contrasty" approach to the lighting design, that employed recessed, low-voltage fixtures fitted with a variety of PAR lamps and installed in a black-painted ceiling. In another instance, a building that was constructed originally to be a power substation in 1923 was transformed into a residence, and the raw, industrial look of the space was retained by using fixtures original to the structure, and electrifying additional selected components.

In the 1950s-built home of a designer/owner, walls were eliminated and playful, eclectic lighting elements—cable systems, small wire-suspended auto tail lights, silver bowl fixtures, sconces and ceiling-mounted luminaires—were added to create a sense of light as a whimsical and magical element. Another architect/owner adapted the lighting specifically to enhance the ambience of each room of his home—an arch of blue neon over a doorway plays against the peach walls of the dining room, and the uplit glassblock in the bedroom illuminates a white-painted niche and provides evening reading light.

An extensive control system and an array of color filters was used throughout a Michigan residence to give the client the flexibility and options he desired. In another case, the interior of a century-old farmhouse has been recreated to resemble Star Trek's U.S.S. Enterprise because the client wanted a space age look. To California clients, a view of the ocean was paramount, and so lighting in their multi-windowed living room comes from recessed sources to avoid glare in the glass walls—circular neon ceiling coves, underlit steps, and sidelit multi-planed walls, and recessed downlights for task and accent lighting.

Artwork is often a featured element in many high-end homes. In one case, an elaborate foyer dome in a Dallas apartment has been fitted with reflector lamps to illuminate artwork. In another home, a flexible system for an art lover was developed that uses a layered lighting sysem—a combination of recessed adjustable units, wall sconces, and portable task lights—that allows occupants to feel comfortable, as well as appreciate the works of art.

In all cases, though a comfortable ambience and adequate task lighting are the basic requirements that need to be met in any residence, there is no one way to design lighting for a particular space. In one home, the quality of light is intentionally varied—in the dining area warmer light from incandescent sources is surrounded by recessed blue-filtered units that cast a cool light in order to draw people around the table.

WHITE LIGHT

Concealed cold cathode wraps around the curved soffit on the second level.

"**T**his house was remodeled—they left about one wall standing," says lighting designer Julia Rezek. The renovated abode included lots of window walls that allowed the client to look out onto the ocean. The house is located on the beach off the Pacific Coast Highway.

The entry area sets the tone for the rest of the home. Glass block columns flank the entry door. "That whole volume of space goes up 30 feet into the air with a skylight at the very top," says Rezek. "The space was lit two ways. Cold cathode wraps up the spiral staircase that goes up four stories. That was quite a feat to detail the cove so it would fit in with the stairs. But the cathode source isn't seen. You see just a very soft wash. And the cold cathode is about 3000 degrees Kelvin, so it's warm.

"The inside of this whole volume of space is lit with color-corrected metal halide. So it's cooler 'inside' and has the warm light wrapping around the stairwell. The contrast in color temperature creates a very interesting effect," says Rezek.

PROJECT LOCATION
Los Angeles, California
LIGHTING DESIGNERS
Julia Rezek and Ray Grenald, Ray Grenald Associates Ltd.
INTERIOR DESIGNERS
Ellen Hoffman and Sharon White, Hoffman White Interiors
PHOTOGRAPHER
Toshi Yoshimi
LIGHTING MANUFACTURERS
Lightolier, Artemide, Express Light, Prudential, Amerlux, Keene, Ron Rezek, Architegraphics, Bega, Halo and Moldcast

General illumination in the entry area is provided by color-corrected metal halide fixtures. A cold cathode cove mimicks the curving of the staircase.

General illumination in the entry area is provided by color-corrected metal halide fixtures. A cold cathode cove mimicks the curving of the staircase.

The metal halide track heads are integrated into the skylight mullions. An additional track unit with a PAR lamp highlights a Steuben glass sculpture that's about 8 feet tall. "Another effect can be created in that space at night by turning all the metal halide units off, so the sculpture is lit with a very tight beam from the incandescent source. That combines with the cove dimly glowing around the stairwell for a very dramatic effect."

Artwork in a niche is lit with two vertically running tracks lamped with PLs. "The client likes a real white light, so we used a lot of sources that were whiter than would usually be used in a residence," Rezek says.

Glass block is also used in the bath. "There is a house adjacent to this one—the houses are just jammed next to each other. The glass block in the bathroom is lit up from the outside of the house," says Rezek. "The unit is bracketed off the side of the house down at the floor level, and aimed to graze the glass block to create a sort of scrim and provide more privacy in the bathroom."

The interior of the bathroom has MR 16s over the tub, and an indirect wall sconce over the mirror that provides diffuse uplight free from shadows and well-suited for grooming tasks.

In the bedroom, wall washers highlight wall-hung artwork. Halogen downlights and low-voltage accent lights also illuminate the space. Again, the halogen light source was selected intentionally to cast a white light. The reading desk area is also lit with the MR 16 fixture, and halogen decorative units are installed by the bed.

By day, the kitchen is flooded with sunlight from extensive windows. By night a combination of recessed and decorative fixtures provides illumination. ''The kitchen is a very tall, narrow space, and it is not separated from the adjacent living space, so when you look at the kitchen you're also looking through to the living room,'' says Rezek. To allow an unobstructed view of the ocean through one of the kitchen's window walls, recessed downlights and wall washers are used.

Good lighting is not just for the rich and famous. Carefully planned lighting effects can add comfort and a feeling of spaciousness to a home without burning a hole in the owner's pocket.

When the owner bought this home in San Francisco, the layout seemed oriented away from allowing inhabitants to enjoy the downtown view of the city. So he flipped the layout around: moved the living room into what was the kitchen, the dining room into the former bathroom, and the kitchen into the former living room.

Potted banana plants look like they are silhouetted in front of the backyard sogi screen, but the plants are actually behind it.

Adding some common sense, but often overlooked, lighting techniques has allowed the owner to achieve his goal of making the interior an inviting place to be. For example, if lighted improperly, reflective or glossy surfaces can cause glare and visual discomfort. But notice the dining room in this home. The cross illumination from ceiling recessed, low-voltage adjustable MR 16 fixtures eliminates glare.

"When you've got a glass top or a high-gloss surface, if the light comes straight down, the glare hits you right back in the face," says lighting designer Randall Whitehead. "But by coming in at a 42 degree angle, you have the illumination without the glare."

The artwork is also highlighted using cross illumination, so there is no reflection of the light source in the glass. The light fixture above the painting on the right is lighting the painting on the left, and vice versa.

In the living room, Nagouchi lanterns and wall sconces create the illusion that they are providing the room's light. In reality each is fitted with only a 15-watt lamp. Though recessed, low-voltage adjustable MR 16 fixtures highlight wall-hung artwork, the ambient illumination comes from a sogi panel wall backlit from the adjacent bedroom.

The glowing wall contributes to a feeling of spaciousness—the person knows there is a room beyond. And the bedroom, which doesn't have a window, seems more open because light filters through from the living room.

A sense of spaciousness is also created in the 8 foot x 8 foot dining area by lighting the exterior deck beyond it, so that visually the deck becomes part of the interior space as well. Two fixtures, mounted outside the home above the four glass panels, are angled to cross illuminate the deck. Each fixture is shielded and holds a 45-watt PAR 38 lamp.

"We are washing the deck with light instead of allowing the light to come straight down and create hot spots," Whitehead says. "We've also added a daylight blue filter to the fixtures. Unlike incandescent light, which has an amber quality to it, the daylight blue filter eliminates the amber and produces a bluer, whiter light so the plants look lush and green."

In the backyard, sogi panels stand 8 feet away from the back of the building. A building mounted quartz fixture projects light toward the back of the panels.

"We can put any object between the back of the panel and the house, and they project the image on the screen," Whitehead says. A bullet-shaped PAR 38 fixture, mounted above the stairway, casts light down through the yucca plant, and grazes the stucco texture of the building wall.

"I like the challenge of working on a remodelling project. Although there are space and budget constraints, we can still do some wonderful things. For example, this backyard is lit with only two fixtures. That effect costs about $350 installed. So there doesn't always have to be a big budget to create a sense of drama," Whitehead says.

PROJECT LOCATION
San Francisco, California
LIGHTING DESIGNER
Catherine Ng and Randall Whitehead, Light Source
ARCHITECT
Mark Thomas
INTERIOR DESIGNER
Christian Wright and Gerald Simpkins, Wright/Simpkins & Co.
ELECTRICAL CONTRACTOR
Dennis Baldwin, Baldwin Electric
PHOTOGRAPHER
Ben Janken, Janken Photography
LIGHTING MANUFACTURERS
Lightolier Inc., Halo Lighting, L'Image, Nagouchi, and Hubbell Inc.

The ambient light in the living room comes from a backlit sogi panel wall (not shown in photo).

Two fixtures illuminate the deck, graze the plants and eliminate hotspots.

The small dining area seems more spacious than it really is because it is visually expanded by the illuminated deck beyond.

BARGAIN BASEMENT

In the entry foyer, the etched glass window on the left looks into the bedroom. Wall sconces brighten the corridor to foster the illusion that it is not a basement apartment.

Good design doesn't have to be expensive, and architect Dhiru Thadani believes that enough to bring in the construction costs for the complete renovation of a one-bedroom, townhouse guest suite in Washington, D.C.'s Georgetown section at $75,000.

The 5 foot, 6 inch high basement had been used originally for coal storage. Before Thadani's clients bought it, previous owners had lowered the floor slab 2 feet. When Thadani was called in to do the renovation, he lowered it several inches again, so the living areas are approximately 7 feet, 10 inches high.

Thadani used several "tricks" to make the space seem open and airy, and as little as possible like a basement. One of them was to flood the apartment with a lot of light—32 fixtures are used, mainly wall sconces, with an array of inexpensive monopoint PAR units in the kitchen.

PROJECT LOCATION
Washington, D.C.
ARCHITECT AND LIGHTING DESIGNER
Dhiru Thadani, AIA, and Peter Hetzel, Thadani Hetzel Partnership
ELECTRICAL CONTRACTOR
Pat McCarty, McCarty Electric Co.
MECHANICAL CONTRACTOR
Mike Didion, Aitken Co.
PAINTING CONTRACTORS
David Goldsborough (light wells), and Fred Jovel (interior)
PLUMBING CONTRACTOR
Warren Blake, Blake & Wilcox
TILE CONTRACTORS
Brian Brennan, Custom Design Tile (floor), and Bob Gray, Ward & Gray (bathroom)
ETCHED GLASS AND MIRRORS
Steve Resnick, Glasscrafters
CUSTOM DOORS AND WINDOWS
Harry Brittain, Culler Construction Co., and Harry Zimmerman, Pioneer Woodworks
CARPET INSTALLATION
John Wilding, Certified Floor Covering
CARPENTERS
Louis Tenenbaum, Miles Brook, Greg Stone, Mykl Messer, and Andre Spenard
MASONS
Charlie Seward, and Paul Howell
PHOTOGRAPHER
Gordon Beall
LIGHTING MANUFACTURERS
Artemide, Conran's, Lightolier, Lutron, Leviton

Most of the fixtures throughout the suite are on dimmers. Units in the entry vestibule, gallery, central hall and dining room can be adjusted up or down. Those in the vestibule and dining room, for example, wash the sculpted ceiling vaults with uplight.

Another inspiration was to repeat a window motif throughout the spaces. For example, as you enter the apartment, an etched glass window separates the hallway/entry vestibule from the bedroom beyond.

"The interior window visually expands the limited space by drawing light from the bedroom windows, and by implying or alluding to a window that opens to an exterior space," says Thadani.

The same concept applies to the kitchen window between the wall-mounted cabinets. It looks into the bathroom beyond.

"And so when you're in the bathroom, you think you've got a window. Natural light comes through indirectly because the bay window opposite that wall in the adjacent living room looks out to the exterior," says Thadani.

Though the photograph shows clear glass, the window was later etched with a pattern based on the four square within a square motif used on etched glass doors, and in the red and gray floor tiles.

Also in the bathroom, two toiletry storage shelf units are shaped like windows, and are fitted with mirrored surfaces that allude to real windows.

The smaller, high-level windows in the kitchen originally had been vents.

"The sidewalk is right up there. The exterior of the building is historically correct and we were not legally allowed to change it because it is in Georgetown. So, those are real windows, that look out onto the sidewalk beyond," says Thadani.

Patterned tiles are used to mark stopping and transition points.

The cabinet on the left conceals the electrical panel. The niche, cabinets and overhead barrel vault give a simple balance and symmetry to the dining room.

The bay window in the living room is an illusion in part. Though the window is about 4 feet, 6 inches deep, only 1 foot, 6 inches of it looks out onto the sidewalk. Three and a half feet are below grade.

"The below grade portion is a light well, and we used a bright white paint on the glass so that the little light that comes in on that northern side of the house bounces around like crazy in the well to make the window seem much brighter than it really is," Thadani says.

In the bedroom, there are another pair of windows. They appear to be of equal size, trimmed at 3 feet, 6 inches each. But in reality, only one is 3 feet, 6 inches. The other is 3 feet square, and partially 'glazed' with painted gypsum board.

"We ran the trim and blinds on the face the same size for both windows as an illusion to get you thinking that thers's lots of windows there," Thadani says. "The reason

A boat builder constructed this central hall library, which conceals a closet, and a staircase that leads to the upper floor.

A large number of light fixtures were intentionally used to bounce as much light as possible off the white walls, and make the apartment seem as unbasement-like as possible.

one is smaller than the other is that there are steps that bring you down to the basement level at the back of the apartment, and what would have been the additional portion of the window is lost because of that.''

Incorporating barrel vaults and lighting them was also part of the plan to give the suite its unbasement-like looks. The barrel vault in the entry hall is uplit with two sconces, and visually frames the window below.

''Basically the vault is set against the direction one travels down the hall. The vault is at a cross axis to the window, and it acts as a stopping or resting place, complemented by the tile carpet on the floor directly underneath it,'' Thadani says.

Another barrel vault has been sculpted into the dining room ceiling.

''All the ducts run in the entry hall to heat and cool the space—that's why the ceiling has been dropped there. But in the dining area, we split the ducts. Instead of having one big, 36-inch wide duct, we made two 18-inch ducts. That left us an open space in the middle of the living and dining areas. So you get a high feeling in the living area, and a kind of framing effect over the dining room table,'' Thadani explains. ''By installing sconces in the vault, it reads from the hallway almost like a skylight, because the two point sources in the curve, by reflection and incidence, cause the light to fall straight down.''

Monopoint fixtures illuminate the small kitchen. The bathroom is on the other side of the window between the cabinets.

Freestanding neon adds a
touch of color to the living
room. The bottom 3 feet,
6 inches of the window is actually below grade.

The basement was originally 5 feet, 6 inches and used for cold storage. Subsequent renovations have increased ceiling height to as much as 7 feet, 10 inches in areas like the living room.

The window in the bathroom looks out into the kitchen. Simple metal and glass sconces uplight the room.

Also in the dining room, the two cabinets with the niche in between creates a Palladian motif—square forms and a semicircle above it. The cabinet on the left was designed to camouflage the electrical panels. The Washington, D.C. electrical code requires that the panel be a maximum of 6 feet away from the meter. The meter is located on the other side of the dining room wall on the building exterior.

Though there is a separate back door entrance, the owners were required to keep the staircase that led to the upper floors, because the townhouse is legally counted as one unit. But to disguise it, Thadani had a custom designed wood library unit constructed by an English boat builder. The curved portion is made of oak flooring; the shelving is mahogany. One side of the unit is a closet; the other side hides the staircase. The shelving is used for books.

Running ducts within the perimeter of the dining room allowed space for the uplit barrel vault in the ceiling center.

PLEATS AND PATTERNS

The added ceiling soffits provided a logical place to hide the air, sound and lighting systems.

A continuing theme throughout this Dallas home is the pleated pattern reminiscent of Oriental origami created by the interior designer Loyd Paxton for wall treatments.

The pleats are played up by the low-voltage lighting system created by lighting designer Craig Roeder.

The interior pleating enhanced by light is clearly seen in the dining room. The wall pleats are actually metal covered with a material that looks like stone. The baseboards are wood. Each pleat is illuminated with a gimbal ring that holds a 25-watt display spot. Each spot is dimmed to about 50 percent. Recessed low-voltage lighting is installed over the dining table.

In the corridor leading to a small bath, more pleated walls are overlaid by lightning bolt patterns made with templates fitted on framing projectors.

The living room uses the pleating in ceiling soffits. Roeder explains how they came to be.

"The apartment in many areas is two stories high, all of them were at a different angle and it was quite ugly. I looked at what Loyd Paxton had done with the pleat design and I made a little model of stalactite type of oragami pleats that hang down and he liked them.

PROJECT LOCATION
Dallas, Texas
LIGHTING DESIGNER
Craig A. Roeder, Craig A. Roeder Associates, Inc.
INTERIOR DESIGNER
Loyd Paxton
PHOTOGRAPHER
Robert Ames Cooks
LIGHTING MANUFACTURERS
Edison Price, Lightolier, Norbert Belfer, Hydrel, Kurt Versen, Strand Controls

"So, in this instance, the lighting designer had the opportunity to get involved in the interiors, because I needed a place for the lighting. You can't recess lights in a sloped ceiling, and I don't like to use track in a residence. And so we designed these floating soffits, which give great scale and interest to the room, and also worked well to house all the air-conditioning, the sound system, and the lighting.

The living room's adjustable accent lights, just like the lighting for the rest of the home, are linked to a control system.

"The whole house has an 18 scene preset dimming system. There is a control station in every room. You can hit a control code of two buttons and control the lighting in the entire house.

"You want to make it as quick and easy for the clients as possible, so they can come home after the opera, for example, and have 15 people over for drinks. They hit two buttons and the whole house goes to a magical setting. And consequently, when they are leaving to go out, they can hit two buttons and turn the whole house off, or turn it to a setting where there's a nightlight or two."

The apartment's ceiling was two stories high in many places and sloped at varying angles. In order to bring some unity to the space, the designers had soffits installed which repeated the ribbed design.

The pleat design is continued throughout the house in the walls and in the ceiling soffits.

Low-voltage accent lights high-light artwork. Cove lighting opens up this little conversation corner.

The illumination is carefully aimed and focused to emphasize the three-dimensionality of antique furnishings and the rich materials of which they are made.

Each pleat is illuminated with a 25-watt display spot dimmed to 50 percent. Recessed low-voltage lamps over the table highlight the zigzag pattern of the table base which mimics the wall pleats.

Pleats are made from metal with a faux stone finish. Illumination expands on the crisp, linear theme of the ribbed elements.

Lightning bolts and stars
provide a sense of dynamic
direction in a corridor that leads
to a small bath.

VILLA VIARE

The clients had an Italian garden wall from a 1920s estate and a ranch house, and they wanted to know what to do with both of them," says architect Alex Gorlin. "So I thought of completing the image of the Italian villa to go with the garden wall."

The clients tore down the ranch house, and built their Italian fantasy complete with villa-like architectural elements—the pergola, the stucco exterior, the terracotta tile roof, and the balanced, Palladian-like symmetry of the structure.

The lighting designed by Cline Bettridge Bernstein Lighting Design, Inc. had two major goals. The first was to highlight artwork—the clients are avid collectors of major contemporary pieces. The second was to use lighting as a decorative element to promote the villa-like styling of the home.

Pools of light distinguish the delicate archways of the delicately balanced mansion.

PROJECT LOCATION
Long Island, New York
LIGHTING DESIGNER
Cline Bettridge Bernstein Lighting Design, Inc.
ARCHITECT
Alex Gorlin, Alex Gorlin Architect
INTERIOR DESIGNER
Paul Siskin
ELECTRICAL CONTRACTOR
Ben Krupenski
PHOTOGRAPHER
Steven Brooke
LIGHTING MANUFACTURERS
Capri Lighting, Edison Price, Harry Gitlin Lighting, Lightolier, Norbert Belfer Lighting

In the entry hall, the tops of the columns are lit with recessed downlights.

Downlights are centered between ceiling beams in the living room, and correspond to the arched window wall panels.

This combination of unobtrusive architectural lighting and visually appealing decorative lighting elements is used throughout the house. For example, the hallway is made inviting by mixing recessed MR 16s to light the tops of columns with a delicately ornate chandelier. In the dining room, quartz wall washers and downlights highlight artwork and another chandelier provides sparkle.

In the living room, a change of pace—PAR 38 wall washers are combined with MR 16 accent lights.

The villa took "just over one year to design and build," Gorlin says. "I knew immediately what I wanted— I had a vision."

The niche in the dining room is illuminated with a single accent light.

The custom designed chandelier in the dining room is fitted with candelabra based lamps.

THE ART OF DRAWING ATTENTION

We wanted guests to stop and take notice, and yet maintain a sense of mystery about how it was accomplished," says lighting designer Randall Whitehead about the dining area of this San Francisco home.

Recessed fixtures have been mounted in the 14-foot high ceiling and are aimed so light travels down through the plants to create dappled patterns. A blue filter has been included to add a silver blue cast to the light, "like shadows on snow" Whitehead says.

This cool light is in contrast to the warmer light from nonfiltered ceiling recessed incandescent units directed toward the base of the pedestal table.

"People are drawn to warm light like a moth to a flame. And so we created this island of warm light surrounded by shadows of cool light to draw them in. We wanted guests to think that all the light was coming from the lantern, but it's not," Whitehead says.

Even though a fireplace is located in the room, it does not work, so a feeling of warmth has been created with light. A track system using PAR 36 lamps enriches the warm gold and burgundy tones in the woods and fabrics of the furnishings.

An "island of warmth" is created in the dining room by surrounding warm incandescent light with cooler, blue-filtered shadows.

PROJECT LOCATION
San Francisco, California
LIGHTING DESIGNER
Randall Whitehead, Light Source
INTERIOR DESIGNER
Eugene Anthony, Eugene Anthony and Associates, Ltd.
ELECTRICAL CONTRACTOR
Kieron Saunders, Saunders Electric
PHOTOGRAPHER
Christopher Irion
LIGHTING MANUFACTURERS
Lightolier Inc., Broesche, Lucifer Lighting Co., Lutron Electronics Co. Inc.

The clients wanted something on the wall above the mantelpiece to draw their guests' attention — but not artwork. So the lighting designer created colored striations by fitting a recessed fixture with pink and blue color filters, and a metal template.

On either side of the fireplace are console tables. To alleviate the dark recesses in those corners, linear incandescent units have been mounted under a 4-inch deep lip at the bottom of each table near the floor. Stone sconces mounted on a pair of columns (not seen in the photographs) bounce light off the ceiling to provide fill light for the room, and to eliminate hard shadow lines on occupants' faces. A dimming system allows the intensity of the lighting to change and the mood of the room at will.

"When we design lighting systems, we make sure each system is flexible," Whitehead says. "It's not like it was in the 1950s — you don't have a sofa, two side tables, a coffee table and an ashtray in the lower left hand corner that remains unmoved. Today, people move their furniture and artwork around all the time, every two or three months, just for a change. So we want the lighting to be able to handle that as well."

To draw out the warm tones of the furnishings, PAR 36 lamps are used in the living room, rather than MR 16s, which would have cast a cooler light.

The "art" on the wall above the fireplace is actually colored striations of light from fixtures fitted with filters and templates.

FOR THE LOVE OF ART

Art is the passion of this San Francisco homeowner. And so a comfortable, flexible lighting system had to be designed to complement the growing and changing collection of oils, pastels, acrylics and sculptures from established and emerging artists that adorns his home.

The lighting designer used layers of light not only to complement the artwork, but to make people feel comfortable in these living spaces. Recessed adjustable MR 16 accent units highlight artworks. The lighting can be changed to accommodate different sized and shaped art objects by installing lamps with different beamspreads.

Pink/orange patterns from MR 16 lamps in the wall sconces create visual interest on the walls, and complement the warm tones of the working fireplace.

Though the eye is drawn to the
stunning artworks in the space,
portable table lamps have been
installed unobtrusively for
people comfort.

PROJECT LOCATION
San Francisco, California
LIGHTING DESIGNER
Randall Whitehead, Light Source
INTERIOR DESIGNER
Owner
ELECTRICAL CONTRACTOR
Earth Electric
PHOTOGRAPHER
Stephen Fridge
LIGHTING MANUFACTURERS
Lightolier Inc., Phoenix Day, Lutron Electronic
Co. Inc.

Lighting for people is provided by wall sconces and task lights. Though the sconces are not custom designed, an MR 16 lamp has been inserted into each one, instead of the usual incandescent bulb. The MR 16's dichroic filter throws out a pink/orange light that is projected from the sconce in a fan shape. So the light and the sconces adorn the walls as kinds of art pieces in themselves.

If you don't look closely at the photos, you might miss the portable task lights. They are intentionally unobtrusive.

"We didn't want the table or reading lamps to overtake the spaces," says lighting designer Randall Whitehead. "These lamps provide good task lighting because they are placed at the right level. The optimum task light comes from between your head and your work or reading surface."

What about ultraviolet rays and art? Whitehead explains, "The reality is that any glass filters out 98 percent of the ultraviolet, leaving only 2 percent. The museums are concerned with this because paintings usually remain illuminated in the same place for long periods of time. There are filters available to eliminate that 2 percent of ultraviolet.

In a home, where the client may be turning the light on for four to six hours each night several nights a week, it's not so critical because the

In the dining area, recessed adjustable MR 16 fixtures accent the painting. Ambient illumination comes from wall sconces.

2 percent of ultraviolet isn't hitting the artwork constantly. But we are working on a project now where the clients are very concerned because the art they own is aged and delicate from the Renaissance, and so we have installed ultraviolet filters on the fixtures,'' Whitehead says.

GIANT LANTERN

Now that the clients' five children were grown and had left home, the couple decided to renovate their 1905-built Carpenter-style house located in Chevy Chase, Maryland. Though the site was beautifully landscaped, with a 200-plus foot deep rear yard complete with running stream, the existing rooms of the house were not open, and did not take advantage of the lovely view.

The design goal for architects Dhiru Thadani, AIA, and Peter Hetzel was to reorient the home to the garden and vice versa. An addition built in the 1930s at the rear of the house was removed, including a small, enclosed sun porch that had been used as a bedroom, to allow a new addition to be constructed in keeping with the style of the house. The roofline and overhang of the new addition is identical to the original. The new interior and exterior details were derived from the original house, and the texture and color of the new stucco was matched.

At the basement level, a two-car garage and workshop were added, per the clients' request. On the first floor, the kitchen was enlarged to include more storage space, and the layout reconfigured to provide for a family room and breakfast area, both of which open directly onto a 12 foot by 30 foot cedar/redwood deck via three pairs of French doors. A symmetrical pair of stairs lead from the deck down to the terrace above the garden.

The kitchen was reconfigured to include room for a sitting area, breakfast table, and family room. Lighting is a combination of pendant fixtures and downlights.

On the second floor, a bath was added, and two existing bedrooms were converted into a study and a dressing room. The new 12 foot by 22 foot master bedroom has windows on three sides. The 17-foot ceiling high-point allowed for an eyebrow window to be placed at the center of the wall facing the garden. A small balcony beyond this window provides an intimate roost above the garden and an expansive link with the landscape.

Eight wall sconces in the sloped-ceiling bedroom make the ceiling appear to float. The wall containing the eyebrow window faces the gardens.

"The addition adds less than 500 square feet of space to the original house," Thadani says. "The $250,000 budget was spent on improving the quality of space, not adding quantity. Mechanical, electrical, and plumbing systems were also improved and updated in the construction process."

The cost of the electrical systems, bringing the residence into conformance with the electrical code, updating the lighting, and lighting the addition and garden came to $25,000. The goal of the lighting design was to provide for both function and change of mood, and was achieved by mixing fixture types and techniques, and including controls.

For example, in the kitchen and family room, incandescent and compact fluorescent lamps are used in a variety of pendant and recessed fixtures and are grouped in separate locations in order to focus on particular activities: the sitting area, breakfast table, sink, food preparation area, and cooking area.

By contrast, the high-sloped ceiling in the master bedroom was softly illuminated with eight wall sconces to make the ceiling appear to float above the floor. This is particularly noticeable at times when the indoor and outdoor light is balanced at dawn and dusk.

Outside the home, fourteen surface-mounted bulkhead fixtures were placed at the balcony, deck and terrace levels. These were grouped in three separate circuits with preset dimmer controls. Low-level landscape fixtures lead the way to the garden. The lush views of the landscape by day are matched by the exterior view of the house from the garden illuminated by night.

"In the evening, viewed from the garden, the addition glows like a giant lantern that spills light over the landscape," says Thadani. "At times the house appears to be a ship steaming across the landscape into the night, with light spilling from the master bedroom/bridge, running light aglow on the deck, and garden lights bobbing in a sea of grass."

This series of photo shows the transformation of the house from day to evening into a giant lantern. The house was renovated to allow it to be more open to the beauty of lush landscape surrounding it.

LOCATION
Chevy Chase, Maryland
LIGHTING DESIGNER AND ARCHITECT
Dhiru A. Thadani, AIA, Peter J. Hetzel, Alan Marko, and Eileen Burke, Thadani Hetzel Partnership, Washington, D.C.
STRUCTURAL ENGINEER
Todd Gerhart, P.E., Structural Engineering Corporation
PHOTOGRAPHER
Dhiru A. Thadani, AIA
LIGHTING MANUFACTURERS
Lightolier, Leviton, Lutron Electronics Co. Inc.

LIGHTING A FINISHED SPACE

What does a lighting designer do when he is called in on a renovation project after it has been completed? Craig Roeder had the chance to find out, when he was approached to relight this Dallas residence without tearing apart the ceiling. (Over $100,000 on paint finishes had already been applied!)

Room after room of the renovated home still retained the original recessed incandescent downlights. What Roeder did was come up with a four-headed fixture that fit into and over the spaces the downlights had occupied.

"We took the old fixture out, mounted a transformer in ceiling plenum that is UL listed, and then covered the downlight hole with the new fixture," Roeder says.

The heads are completely adjustable, and contain Osram 50-watt 10 degree lamps. Since a couple of circuits existed in each room for the downlights, the new fixtures were equipped with control settings as well.

The multi-headed fixture allows the variety of sculptures and artworks in the entry hall to be highlighted.

PROJECT LOCATION
Dallas, Texas
LIGHTING DESIGNER
Craig A. Roeder, Craig A. Roeder Associates, Inc.
INTERIOR DESIGNER
Joyce Wynn
ELECTRICAL CONSULTANT
Rick Spaulding, Litelab
PHOTOGRAPHER
Robert Ames Cook
LIGHTING MANUFACTURERS
Litelab, Osram, Lutron Electronics Co. Inc.

"In the kitchen, there were so many holes in the ceilings that we decided we didn't want to install four-headed fixtures, so I just modified the fixture and used two-headed versions," Roeder says. To add to the fun of the pastel painted kitchen, the designer installed purple neon above the kitchen cabinets.

Summing up the challenge and accomplishment of this project, Roeder says, "We took a set of parameters that were almost impossible to deal with, and still lit the house well."

Darkened walls and highly focused pools of light create high drama in the living room.

Fixtures are placed where the standard incandescent down-lights used to be, since the lighting designer could not open the finished ceiling.

Filters fitted to the fixtures above the shelves in the bar area turn the crystal a rich cobalt blue.

The rich materials used in this home — like the marble tile floors, specially painted walls, and custom carpeting — are worthy of notice, and get it thanks to highlighting from the new lighting system.

Beamspreads are so precisely
focused that individual objects
seem to glow on their own.

In the kitchen, two-headed fixtures have been installed where
the incandescent downlights
used to be because there were
so many of them. A single row
of purple neon has been installed above the cabinets.

The four-headed fixtures high-light art objects placed through-out the bedroom and on the shelves.

Table lamps for reading have been placed on either side of the bed. The same four-headed fixture used throughout the house is seen again here in the bedroom.

CALIFORNIA COMFORT

The owner of this Belevedere, California home, built in the 1950s, decided to do an extensive renovation. This included replacing the big, sliding glass doors that bordered an outdoor landscaped garden with French doors, and taking out the 8 foot ceilings and leaving the open beam construction exposed.

"The ceilings all soared in there," says lighting designer Randall Whitehead. "We wanted to fill all those areas with a comfortable light, so as one travels from room to room, there is a consistency of look and feel. We didn't want it to be so much a lighting statement as much as we wanted it to be a comfortable environment."

Wall sconces with cool quartz sources form the capitals of columns in the living room. Warm linear incandescent tubes are recessed in the sill of the faux windows above the columns.

In the living room, the lighting designer worked with the architect and interior designer to create faux columns topped by wall sconces that acted as the capitals. The sconces include asymmetric reflectors which throw the light out toward the center of the room, instead of allowing it, as a standard sconce would, to be cast straight up. This also requires fewer fixtures to be used to light up a large space.

Whitehead notes that clients are often concerned that wall sconces will use up space that could be adorned by artwork. So, in this case, the fewer number of fixtures opened up some of the walls for the display of art.

Adjacent to the living room is the dining area. Miniature track fixtures have been mounted on the sides of the exposed ceiling beams, rather than on the under side of the beams.

"By mounting them on the sides, the beam acts as a natural baffle, so you have all the flexibility of the track system or a recessed adjustable system without having to see it," says Whitehead.

In the small faux clerestory windows above the columns and sconces, a linear incandescent source has been recessed into the bottom sill. The incandescent light source produces an amber light with its higher color temperature, and a pleasing contrast to the quartz-sourced sconces. The clerestory windows visually recede to create a greater sense of depth and interest in the space.

PROJECT LOCATION
Belvedere, California
LIGHTING DESIGNER
Randall Whitehead, Light Source
INTERIOR DESIGNER
Linda Bradshaw-Allen
ELECTRICAL CONTRACTOR
Dennis Baldwin, Baldwin Electric
PHOTOGRAPHER
Ben Janken, Janken Photography
LIGHTING MANUFACTURERS
Halo Lighting, Lightolier Inc., Alkco Lighting
Inc., Loran, Lutron Electronics Co. Inc.

The owner opted to tear out the previously existing 8 foot ceiling and leave the open beam construction exposed.

The asymmetric reflector in the sconces throws light out into the center of the room. This means fewer fixtures can be used to illuminate the room, and walls can be freed up for artwork.

The illumination in this photo comes from the wall sconces — it is not photographer's fill light. The French doors open out onto a landscaped garden.

In the bathroom, sconces mounted on either side of the vanity cast soft illumination for grooming.

"I like finding nooks and crannies in which to hide lights," says Whitehead. And he's done that in the tub area. The beam above the bathtub is actually a support truss and a hollow trough. Fluorescent tubes have been installed in it along with a fascia board on the underside to hide the tubes and the wiring.

"This fills the area with a clean, creamy white light," Whitehead says, "and creates the illusion the light is coming from a skylight, but there is no skylight."

Recessed in the support beam above the shower is a fluorescent fixture.

Sconces provide soft sidelighting for grooming at the vanity.

LIGHT MAGIC

PROJECT LOCATION
Dallas, Texas
LIGHTING DESIGNERS
Tully and Kalynn Weiss, Tully Weiss
Lighting Design
PHOTOGRAPHERS
James F. Wilson and Richard Pruitt
LIGHTING MANUFACTURERS
Ingo Maurer, Lite Cycle, Edison Price,
Sentinel Silver Bowl fixtures by Tully Weiss &
Ron Wommack, Lighting Services Inc. (color
media), Miniature Lighting Products, Tinker
Toy Fixture by Tully Weiss, IPI, Lazin Lighting,
Artemide

Low partitions have replaced
full walls and create a sense of
openness while maintaining
some sense of intimacy within
each space.

ight is a magical thing and sometimes doesn't take a whole lot of effort to create and enjoy," says lighting designer Tully Weiss, who with Kalynn Weiss transformed their 1950s-built "crackerbox" house into a playful collection of open, airy spaces.

Though details from the original house were kept—like the swirl-patterned ceiling in the living room —in some areas, full walls have been eliminated in favor of low partitions. For example, between the living room and dining areas, the partitions serve several purposes. They allow occupants to see into other areas of the house, yet maintain some sense of closeness and intimacy, and serve as built-in book shelves.

Fixtures above the table are called Sentinel and have been designed by Tully Weiss and Ron Wommack.

In other areas of the home, walls have been eliminated completely. For example, two adjacent bathrooms and a small closet have been re-modeled into one large 10-foot by 10-foot bath with two sinks and a tub.

The lighting scheme of the home is eclectic, but the overriding theme is a sense of fun and whimsy. Cable systems, small wire suspended auto-mobile tail lights, recessed and silver bowl fixtures, sconces, and ceiling mounted luminaires are combined to create visual surprises as well as provide adequate task lighting.

"When you look at the stars in a clear sky, there's something magical about those pinpoints of light. So whether you use little low-voltage lamps, or any type of lamp that create a spangling effect in an open space or corner, it elicits a response that reminds one of being a child. It's playing with light. Life is real serious, and it's nice to relax a little at times," says Weiss, who has chosen to relax at home with his own magical pinpoints of light.

Bleachers in the entertainment area are used for reading books, sipping coffee, or enjoying the view of the garden outside.

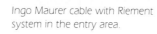
Ingo Maurer cable with Riement system in the entry area.

The cable system is by Ingo Maurer. The ceiling-mounted fixture is a Sputnik vintage fixture purchased from a 1950s store in Dallas.

The entertainment area looks
out onto the exterior gardens.

The kitchen, outfitted with a vintage stove, cabinets and stainless steel countertops, is equipped with dimmers that allow the owners to vary the intensity of the light.

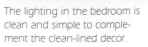
The lighting in the bedroom is clean and simple to complement the clean-lined decor.

Wall-mounted fixtures and downlights provide light for grooming that's fun to look at, too.

DECORATING WITH LIGHT

In this exterior view, light floods through the loggia of the rear addition.

A 3,000 square foot Georgian Revival style home was what these New Orleans clients, avid art and antique collectors, purchased after a fire destroyed their previous home and priceless possessions. The Georgian structure underwent a complete renovation and was expanded, with additions on the south side and rear of the house.

"The lighting concept was twofold," says lighting designer Francesca Bettridge. "First, the lighting plan used the color of the sources and patterns of light to reinforce the composition of the architecture.

"The second major aspect of the lighting concept," Bettridge says, "was to decorate the house with light. The clients are avid collectors, and since they were literally starting over, their collection constantly grows and changes."

In the central hallway, open reflector downlight wall washers fill narrow volumes of space and wash the walls. Small aperture MR 16 accent lights installed in the vaulted, pitched ceiling cast tight beams through the crystal chandeliers and onto the floor.

In the living room on the stair hall side, PAR 38 accent lights with spread lenses illuminate the growing and changing art collection.

Illumination for the kitchen includes undercounter 25T6-1/2 strips used in combination with open reflector downlights and wall washers.

The highlights of the master bedroom is an incandescent cove that defines the spatial element of the room.

PROJECT LOCATION
New Orleans, Louisiana
LIGHTING DESIGNER
Cline Bettridge Bernstein Lighting Design, Inc.
ARCHITECT AND INTERIOR DESIGNER
Concordia Architects
PHOTOGRAPHER
Tina Freeman, Decatur Studio
LIGHTING MANUFACTURERS
Capri Lighting, Edison Price

In the master bath, shadowless light ideal for grooming tasks comes from linear incandescent lamps placed behind the six-foot-long mirror on all four sides. The perimeter of the one-piece mirror has been sandblasted to allow even, diffuse light to come through (the lamps are turned off in the photograph). The lamps can be accessed from the closet beyond.

A fluorescent cove in the skylight well provides general illumination at night.

Besides a south side screened porch, a 1,800 square foot addition at the rear of the house was made that opens onto a terrace. The glassed-in loggia's French doors open to allow occupants of interior rooms to look into the terrace, which, in turn, overlooks the garden and pool.

The terrace is lit by floor washers, as well as by quartz wall washers situated at the French doors that throw light onto the terrace in the distinctive pattern of the glass panes. Recessed PAR 38 downlights cast light onto the faux marble columns that are crowned with terra-cotta capitals.

''The lighting responds to the architecture,'' says Bettridge, ''organizing the spaces, and also to the owners, and their love of the precious and the whimsical.''

PAR 38s with spread lenses illuminate the changing collection in the living room on the stairwell side.

Open reflector downlight shoot down through the chandelier lighting crystal and putting light on the table.

Downlight/wallwashers light the wall between the living room and library.

SPACE AGE SANCTUARY

In the library, recessed open reflector A-lamp downlights provide light for those reading or conversing at the same time bringing out the luxury of the glove leather banquettes.

A space-age, 21st century environment was what the owner wanted to be housed, by contrast, in a Federalist mansion built in 1748 and located on fifteen acres northwest of Philadelphia. An innovative interior was created by juxtaposing diverse materials and elements—fine glove leathers and soft cashmeres with industrial metals and finishes.

The goals for the lighting system designed by Cline Bettridge Bernstein Lighting Design, Inc. included using existing equipment in an innovative way to satisfy the unique design requirements of the owner and designer, highlighting the colors, finishes and textures of the rich

materials, enhancing the illusions of space created by the architecture and interior design, providing flexibility to change mood and create drama with an economical dimming system, and overcoming the structural limitations inherent in a two centuries old-plus structure.

Creative illusions begin in the entry foyer which contains a staircase made grand by lining the wall with mirrors. Adjustable MR 16 fixtures recessed in the underside of the staircase to the third floor are focused to stream light down the center of the stairwell simulating shafts of daylight coming from the actual staircase above.

PROJECT LOCATION
Philadelphia, Pennsylvania
LIGHTING DESIGNER
Cline Bettridge Bernstein Lighting Design, Inc.
ARCHITECT
Eric Bernard (deceased), Eric Bernard Designs
PHOTOGRAPHER
Peter Aaron/ESTO
LIGHTING MANUFACTURERS
Capri Lighting, Edison Price, Harry Gitlin
Lighting, Lightolier

The structure of the low 7 foot, 6 inch ceilinged living room eliminated the option of using recessed fixtures. So instead, track is recessed along the edges of two sections of the stepped ceiling with small remote-transformed MR 16 fixtures. The perforated fixture housing adds sparkle to the room, along with the interplay of light with the silver-leaf ceiling detail. Fluorescent strip uplights placed behind the banquette are mirrored by a low-voltage strip recessed beneath the seating.

In the library, each burgundy-lacquered shelf is lighted with a frosted C-lamp strip. Objects on shelves are accented with R-14 lamps. The fine quality of the glove leather banquettes is brought out by recessed open reflector A-lamp downlights that provide task lighting for reading.

The ribbed glass surface-mounted fixtures used in the kitchen were developed originally for exterior use. Light from those units highlights the semi-specular copper strips of the cabinets. At the same time, the lens on the bottom side of the fixtures spreads illumination evenly over the work surfaces. Task light is provided also by incandescent T-lamp strips mounted under the cabinetry. Ambient light over the sink area comes from recessed open reflector A-lamp downlights.

The challenge of lighting almost black rooms was presented in the master bedroom and bath/exercise areas. The sound-proofed bedroom has an unusual space age canopy bed marked by a double coved structure that rises on one wall, travels across the width of the room and then descends on the other wall to frame the fireplace. Remote-ballasted fluorescents furnish the glow that makes the structure seem to float. Low-voltage strips are also recessed under the bed and massage couch. Monopoint MR 16 fixtures provide added accent light because there was no available depth in which to recess fixtures. The drum at the bed contains the device for controlling all the light fixtures in the house.

The closet is illuminated with fluorescent strips recessed into the floor and covered by a metal grill work. The light is picked up by chrome strips framing the passageway and seems to create a tunnel of light. The cedar-lined closet contains a cleaner's revolving rack that is lighted by color-corrected fluorescents and switched on when the voice activated door is opened.

In the kitchen, the fixtures had been designed for exterior application and so their use in the kitchen is unexpected and adds to the "theater" of the space.

In the master bedroom, recessed open reflector A-lamp downlights highlight art in the windows.

In the closet, fluorescent strips are recessed into the floor and covered by a metal grill work.

The midnight blue TV room beyond the exercise room uses recessed open reflector A-lamp downlights for general illumination.

The bath/exercise area is covered in a shiny black ribbed ceramic tile. To highlight the sheen and texture of the material, a low-voltage bollard has been installed to throw light across the floor and skim the tile surface. Another bollard has been specially modified to be suspended from the ceiling to skim the surface of the ceiling tile as well.

Illumination for grooming at the sink comes from vertical incandescent tubes. General illumination in the midnight blue television room comes from recessed open reflector A-lamp downlights.

Within a limited budget, the designer had to create a fantasy room for the client's teenage daughters who would visit on occasion. The room has gauzelike material draped between aluminum columns which have been modified to become lighting fixtures. Rectangular holes were cut in the sides of the columns facing the walls at the top and bottom. Each column was outfitted with two R-lamps: one white, and the other a color. Low-voltage strip lights are used under the platforms.

The control system allows fixtures to be controlled from a variety of locations, as well as from a master computer. A carrier current system interfaced with a standard wall box switch/dimmer was used as a flexible and economical solution.

FLOWING LIKE OCEAN WAVES

Since Robert Ross was responsible for the architecture, interior design and lighting design of this remodeled, 2,500 square foot Malibu home, he was able to envision lighting as an integral design element from the start of the project.

The wall containing the artwork is actually composed of two panels. The artwork hung on the back panel is sidelighted by fixtures concealed behind the edges of the front panel.

"No matter where you sit in the living room, you have a view," says Ross. The owners wanted to be able to relax and enjoy the ocean view not only during the day, but at night as well. To minimize reflections in the window walls of interior furnishings, Ross intentionally avoided portable and decorative fixtures, and instead relied on concealed and recessed sources. Exterior foreground landscape elements also have been illuminated to reduce reflections and to add a natural aesthetic beauty to the view.

PROJECT LOCATION
Malibu, California
ARCHITECTURE, INTERIOR AND
LIGHTING DESIGN
Robert Ross Inc. — Robert Ross, president, Eric Furan, associate
PHOTOGRAPHER
David Glomb — David Glomb Photography
LIGHTING MANUFACTURERS
American Neon, Capri Lighting, Lucifer Lighting Co., Sentinel Lighting, Sylvan Designs Inc., Lutron Electronics Co. Inc.

The lower level of the living room is at the front of the house, and is distinguished by a window wall and ceiling for unimpeded ocean viewing.

"The owner liked the idea of geometric shapes, and we discussed the positioning of round elements," says Ross. "Once I set up the large circle in the living room, all the forms grew and became defined from that."

What Ross calls "layers of light" accentuate and enhance the flowing forms that intersect vertically and horizontally.

"I usually design a lighting system in layers: low levels equivalent to candlelight for relaxing; ambient and fill light; and task and accent light," Ross explains.

The living room is built on two levels. The upper level is defined by a circular ceiling cove that contains two skylights. The shaft above the fireplace runs vertically up through one of the skylights. The other skylight is recessed in the opposite side of the cove.

The circular soffit is lit with neon concealed in its perimeter. Additional task and accent lighting is provided by 50-watt, MR 16 downlights, some of which can be individually switched. The locations of these task lights was determined in conjunction with the client.

The non-window wall in this area is composed of two unconnected, overlapping panels. The back panel contains artwork sidelighted with strips concealed behind the front

The upper level of the living room is defined by a soffit illuminated with concealed neon.

Colored shadow-play is created in the foliage outside the bedroom window by a mercury vapor luminaire fitted with a blue-green filter.

panel. Recessed downlights also accent the artwork, as well as create scallop patterns along either side of the front panel.

Steps leading down to the lower level are underlit with neon. This level, at the front of the house, is surrounded by an all-glass wall and ceiling ideal for ocean viewing.

Low-voltage lighting was chosen for its appropriate color temperature, focusability, and good switching and dimming control. All the lights are dimmable.

"I build in controls to integrate all functions, and to allow clients to create special relationships; that is, to emphasize their preference in what they can choose to see; and, as a result, feel," Ross says.

The house had originally been ranch style, with the roof sloped at a slight angle. In the bedroom, the white ceiling is peaked, and up-lighted by a continuous line-voltage strip of candelabra-based lamps placed at 6 inches on center. Vertical strip lights are placed next to the art-work at the head of the bed to high-

The swirling, winding staircase mimicks the rounded forms of the structure and furnishings of the living room.

Recessed fixtures were chosen to eliminate glare in the windows that would have been caused by decorative or portable luminaires. Here's a window at the side of the house. You can see how the window wall and ceiling of the front facade slopes outward.

A low-voltage spotlight highlights artwork in the niche.

light the overlapping wall panels. Low-voltage recessed pinspots are located throughout the room for task lighting. The bed platform is visually floated by low-voltage strip lights mounted beneath it.

"Using layers of light insures choice, and human contentment with the environment influenced by one's ability to control light," Ross says.

In the bedroom, the multi-planed wall and platform are floated with low-voltage strip lights.

A portion of the peaked ceiling in the bedroom is illuminated with a continuous strip of line-voltage candelabra-based lamps placed at 6 inches on center.

SHOWCASING ANTIQUES

The second floor of the building that houses the Loyd-Paxton Galleries in Dallas is actually the residence of the gallery owners. And the residence contains antique furnishings that are just as unique and valuable as those sold on the floor below.

Lighting designer Craig Roeder had to devise a lighting system that would showcase objects and furniture that were once the possessions of royalty like Napolean and Josephine, and Marie Antoinette, and yet be livable for the owners.

The building exterior is illuminated with burial units that contain 150-watt quartz PAR 38 lamps.

"One day Charles Paxton Gremillion turned to me during the design process of this entire building," Roeder recounts, "and said, 'What color would make the lighting go away as much as possible?' I looked at him and said, 'Black'. But who would ever have thought of doing it? Two days later he said, 'I've got it all figured out. We're doing a black ceiling.' And it works. He pulled it off."

In those unobtrusive black ceilings, the lighting designer recessed low-voltage fixtures fitted with a variety of PAR 36, some very narrow spots, and some quartz fixtures for the large murals. Before the lighting was installed, the owners carefully placed the furniture and antiques, so the illumination would fall only where it was needed.

The second floor terrace overlooks downtown Dallas. The custom designed exterior uplights are installed flush with the flooring and are fitted with black louvers to prevent light from reaching the eyes of any passersby. The exterior of the building is painted a neutral taupe. The owners can install color filters on special occasions to give the building a festive air.

The interior lighting systems are controlled by a sophisticated computer system. Each circuit in the house, gallery and exterior can be dimmed simultaneously from any control station. Each room can be dimmed independently as well from its own control panel.

The client opted to have the ceiling painted black so the lighting would be as unnoticeable as possible. Dramatic pools of light in the living room and library focus attention on the antique furnishings.

Recessed low-voltage units
highlight the gilded frame and
marble table in the dining area.

The winding stairs are underlit with low-voltage strip lights.

In the bar area, filters on fixtures make the ice and crystal
glow purple.

Color filters added to the recessed exterior fixtures add a
festive air to the building on
holidays or when the clients are
entertaining.

PROJECT LOCATION
Dallas, Texas
LIGHTING DESIGNER
Craig A. Roeder, Craig A. Roeder
Associates, Inc.
ARCHITECT
Paul Pedigo, Hendricks and Wall
INTERIOR DESIGNERS
Charles Paxton Gremillion and Loyd Ray Taylor
PHOTOGRAPHER
Robert Ames Cook
LIGHTING MANUFACTURERS
Norbert Belfer, Edison Price Inc., Hydrel,
Litelab, Alesco, Sylvan Designs, Strand Controls

THE POWER HOUSE

When the owner requested a minimalist approach be taken and a limited budget be used to convert a power substation originally built in 1923 into a private residence, the key to the success of the lighting design became attention to detail.

"It's such a high-tech looking space. When you do something like this, and leave all the conduit bare, it has to be highly crafted by the electrician and general contractor. You can't just have a typical electrician come in and wire it up. Everything had to be precise and clean," says Pamela Hull Wilson, lighting designer for the project who worked closely with Gary Cunningham, the architect and interior designer on carrying through the design concept. "So many houses are built today and they caulk to fit. In this one, you couldn't get away with any of that because everything's exposed."

Though the function of the building was changed, the goal was to maintain the historic feel by using fixtures that were original to the building, and electrifying existing components to act as fixtures.

The focal points on the building exterior are The Dallas Power & Light entry sign and the incoming service wires highlighted with a weather proof fluorescent strip. Blue and green PL lamps playfully simulate power leaking out, and projected porcelain reflectors create an even band of illumination.

Inverted silver-bowl lamps mounted on the roof cast light down through the skylights to the third floor music room, and also provide exterior deck illumination. The whimsical quality on the facade reappears on the roof with three penthouses highlighted as sculptural elements and red flashing lights mimicking downtown skyscrapers.

The interior layout has the dining area, living room and kitchen on the first floor; a railed mezzanine that looks down into the first floor living area; and an open, hardwood third floor, used as a music room, that is reached by a glass elevator.

The vertical planes of the first floor living areas are emphasized with light from surface-mounted adjustable incandescent fixtures.

On the second and third stories, a portion of the illumination comes through a row of frosted glass panels interlaced with steel netting in the floor.

"The original cable trenches, which could be accessed from the top or the bottom, were covered with steel plates. So, the steel plates were pulled off, and the power trench was taken out, and frosted, steel-netted glass has been installed where the steel had been," Wilson says. "We wanted to uplight the glass so a definite light source couldn't be seen. We drew from the design concepts

Inverted silver-bowl lamps on the roof cast illumination down through the skylights to the third floor interior, and provide deck illumination.

PROJECT LOCATION
Dallas, Texas
LIGHTING DESIGNER
Pamela Hull Wilson, Lighting Consultant
ARCHITECT AND INTERIOR DESIGNER
Gary Cunningham
ELECTRICAL CONTRACTOR
MEP Systems
PHOTOGRAPHER
James F. Wilson
LIGHTING MANUFACTURERS
LSI Lighting Systems, Hubbell Inc., Osram Corp., Stonco Lighting, Lazin Lighting Inc., Artemide Inc.

that were already at hand, which included the reflector lamps up on the third floor, and bought new white porcelain reflectors, and fitted them with silver-bowled lamps."

During the daytime, the glass troughs become internal skylights, filtering light from the third floor skylights.

The third story has a combination of general and accent lighting. Uplight in the music room is provided by original porcelain housings with silver-bowl lamps, and by incandescent lamps housed in sheet metal scoops. The junction boxes accept clamp-on incandescent accent lights for use on special occasions. The general illumination comes from the exterior-illuminated skylights.

The industrial look of the project extends even to the controls. They are mounted in gray metal boxes and are line voltage with industrial toggle switches.

Suspended track fixtures furnish illumination over the table in the library on the first floor.

The third floor is used for chamber music. Illumination comes from exterior-lighted skylights, and incandescent uplights.

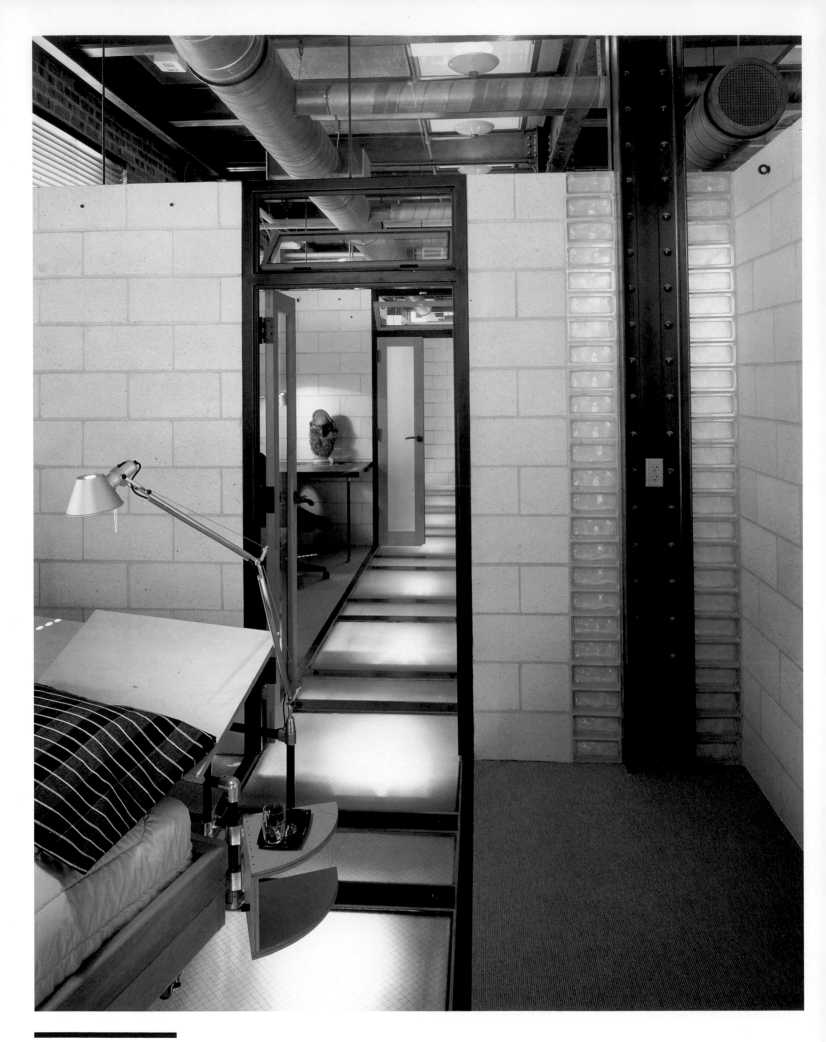

In the living areas, wire-meshed
glass troughs are uplighted
from below with silver-bowl
reflector lamps.

TALL TOWER

This Shingle Style home designed by architect Robert Stern is an always-interesting collection of dormer windows and projecting bays, and a gambrel roof combined with classical Tuscan columns and full entablatures. Given this traditional styling, the lighting designed by Cline Bettridge Bernstein Lighting Design Inc. had to be subtle, but architecturally enhancing.

The achievement of this goal can be seen immediately at the entrance. Concealed, weatherproof exterior incandescent strip lights gently uplight the barrel vaulted outdoor portico smoothly and evenly. Decorative lanterns on either side of the door add sparkle and emphasize the classical balance of the architectural elements.

Warm, incandescent sources were purposefully chosen to enhance the colors of interior furnishings, and to promote an inviting, beckoning feeling when the home, situated on a Long Island waterfront site, is viewed from a distance. The golden glow is most striking emanating from the octagonal two-story tower reminiscent of a seaside lighthouse.

PROJECT LOCATION
Long Island, New York
LIGHTING DESIGNER
Cline Bettridge Bernstein Lighting Design, Inc.
ARCHITECT AND INTERIOR DESIGNER
Robert A.M. Stern Architects
ELECTRICAL CONTRACTOR
Gary and Charles Knoebel
PHOTOGRAPHER
William Choi
LIGHTING MANUFACTURERS
Edison Price, Lightolier, Norbert Belfer
Lighting, Sentinel Lighting

The first floor room is illuminated with a low-voltage cove that makes the wall and ceilings glow. The second floor, which houses a playroom for the client's daughter, is illuminated with a pendant lantern style fixture centrally placed in the conical trussed ceiling. "A lantern effect is created because the light emanates from the inside of the tower out," says lighting designer Francesca Bettridge.

The unobtrusive, clean character of the lighting is even continued into the bath, where linear custom columns of glass and bronze have been designed to provide uniform overall illumination for grooming tasks. The incandescent coves contain T10 lamps. The lighting controls are located in a panel behind the door that leads to the bath.

The house from a distance reveals the purposeful choice of warm color rendering light sources for the interior.

Incandescent strip lights uplight the barrel vault at the entry.

Fixtures in the bath were custom made from etched glass and brass and fitted with linear incandescent lamps.

LIFE ON A STAGE

The exterior of the home has a sculptured, multi-layered, geometric feel.

Because the owner of this 5,800 square foot custom home in Bloomfield Hills, Michigan entertains frequently, he required a lighting system capable of great flexibility and of producing very dramatic effects. The two and a half story home, which is built on a lake, is well windowed, so by day there is a lot of daylight contribution.

Drama begins at the entrance with colored light. "The MR 16 fixtures recessed down into a soffit at the top of the entrance door have linear glass spread lenses and blue filters to evenly illuminate the stepped soffit area," says lighting designer Stefan Graf.

Far shot and closeup of grand hallway using recessed downlights. The emphasis is on the architectural lines and not on distracting decorative fixtures.

The multi-planed living room continues the look of the exterior.

Projections, spotlighting, color filters, and precise aiming create contrast and drama in the informal living areas of the suburban home.

In the main entrance and living room, a variety of light sources and fixture types are integrated into the voluminous space. Recessed adjustable MR 16s with light blue color filters wash the marble at the top of the winding staircase. Low-voltage edgelighting is also used underneath the handrail that wraps around the spiral staircase and illuminates the stairway.

Artwork in the living room is highlighted with recessed, adjustable MR 16 units. In the fountain area, low voltage quartz lighting is used with red color filters that wash the marble behind the statue.

An indirect lighting system includes a series of 200-watt PAR 46 fixtures and 90-watt PAR 38 lamps fitted with different color filters that can make the ceiling glow white, lavender, peach. The programmable electronic low-voltage control system allows time crossfades to a number of different scenes in the soffit that wraps around the living room.

Template projectors have also been installed in the room. The owner can insert stainless steel templates—such as clouds, stars, holiday symbols—in combination with color washes to create a customized light show.

Color filters and flexible controls allows a variety of moods to be created in the living room.

The dining room is adjacent to the living room. The bar is illuminated with recessed adjustable MR 16 fixtures fitted with daylight blue filters to give the crystal glassware an unusual, cool character that contrasts with the warm, incandescent lighting in the rest of the space. Indirect, dimmable fluorescent cove lighting has been included to provide ambient illumination.

Differences in lighting technique
change the look and moods of
the space. Note, for example,
the way the wall sculpture is
grazed and the colors rendered.

Sculpture highlighted with MR 16 downlights surround the top and bottom of the winding staircase. The perimeter of the flooring which circles around the stairs is fitted with recessed tubelights.

The mirrored master bath contains recessed, adjustable MR 16 units as well that cast pools of light on plants, a vase and art objects in a cabinet. The blue light emanating from the soffit above the whirlpool tub is produced by a compact fluorescent source fitted with a blue filter that is placed outside the skylight.

Edgelighting is accomplished with low-voltage track. Varied lighting fixtures focused on the mosaic allow for changes in effects produced. MR 16 units with linear spread lenses also light the sculpture from the top and sides.

The den is lit indirectly from a soffit with 75 R 30 lamps. Recessed, adjustable MR 16 units light the wall-hung artwork and the table in the center of the room.

Sculptures in the recreation room are also highlighted with recessed MR 16s fitted with gold filters. The warm feeling complements the sculptures, which have a bronze character to them. One sculpture has been backlit, and the other is front lit.

In the kitchen, under-cabinet lighting supplies countertop task light. MR 16 units light the countertops by the sink and the table in the breakfast nook. A row of twinkle lights has been built into the mullions. This 12-volt lamp and socket system was installed at the crosspoint to the window mullion to add some sparkle to the view out at night.

PROJECT LOCATION
Lansing, Michigan
LIGHTING DESIGNER
Stephen Graf, Illuminart
ARCHITECT
Jack Brown, Brown and Deyo
INTERIOR DESIGNER
Richard Talbert
LANDSCAPE ARCHITECT
John Crampton
PHOTOGRAPHERS
Thomas Weschler, and Balthazar Korab
LIGHTING MANUFACTURERS
Capri Lighting, Devon, GE Lighting, Gray Glass Co., Kurt Versen, Lee, Litelab, Lite-Touch, Lithonia, Osram, Special FX, and Tivoli

ROW HOUSE RENOVATION

All the walls have been painted soft pastel colors, and all ceilings, trims and moldings have been painted white not only to highlight detail and relief, but to add to the open, spacious feel of the interiors.

This 1,800 square foot house was built in 1923 and is at the end of a run of row houses in Washington, D.C.'s Georgetown section. The owner, architect Dhiru Thadani, in the course of renovating, designed into each room a central element or focal point, and an ambience that could be altered by flexible lighting systems.

The living room, for example, had previously been illuminated by a single glass globe mounted in the center of the ceiling. Thadani replaced the globe with a ceiling fan, and installed some simple, but unusual lighting treatments. On either side of the windows at the front of the house sit speakers for the stereo system. Outdoor fixtures each holding one, 150-wat PAR lamp have been concealed behind the speakers.

"The PAR lamps make the speakers literally act as sconces, because the upper sections of the speakers are translucent metal mesh, and the light shines through them to the rest of the room," Thadani says.

Tizio decorative fixtures one on either side of the "momma and poppa" chairs, provide task light for reading and for browsing through wall-mounted shelves that hold records and compact discs.

PROJECT LOCATION
Washington, D.C.
ARCHITECT AND LIGHTING DESIGNER
Dhiru Thadani, AIA, and Peter Hetzel,
Thadani Hetzel Partnership
PHOTOGRAPHER
Gordon Beall and William Mills
LIGHTING MANUFACTURER
Conran's

All eyes are drawn to the end
of the living room, which is
illuminated simply with two
outdoor fixtures placed behind
boxy meshed speakers on either
side of the room.

"The wonderful thing about the house is that the living room, the dining room and the sun room beyond all align," Thadani says. "With the French doors open and the back door open you can see all the way through the house. On one end of the axis, we have the speakers with the two lights behind them. I felt the dining room needed some emphasis to reinforce the axis that runs through the house."

A thin arch of blue neon, that glows in striking contrast to the creamy pink walls, has been installed above the French doors in the dining room. The wiring for the neon is run through the walls and down to the basement, where the transformer is located. The transformer's remote placement eliminates any "hum" from the neon in the dining area. The neon is equipped with a low-voltage dimmer, so the color can be intensified or softened, depending on time of day and occasion.

In the master bedroom, the focal point is a freestanding, U-shaped wall that divides the room into two zones: the sleeping area, and a walk-in closet. The sleeping area is marked by an uplighted border of glassblock behind the headboard of the bed. The light from the glassblock illuminates the recessed arched niche above it.

"The walls are pink, but the niche behind the bed is painted white. The thickness of the glassblock allows only the niche to be lighted, with no spill light cast out into the rest of the room. So if one person is sleeping, the room still feels dark, but if the other person is holding a newspaper up, it can be read comfortably," Thadani says.

The cove was originally lamped with incandescents, but Thadani has replaced them with PLs. One portion of the glassblock unscrews for easy relamping.

One downlight highlights objects in the niche next to the bed, which had been a shallow closet before the renovation.

The freestanding wall, behind which the clothes are stored, contains two glassblock "eyes". Four bulkhead fixtures have been mounted on the closet side of the wall relatively high, so that light from them shines through the glass block and over the top of the wall to gently fill the room.

In the dining room, the sweeping blue neon over the archway, together with the Le Corbusier LC/6 dining table and LC/7 swivel chairs establish a style reminiscent of a diner.

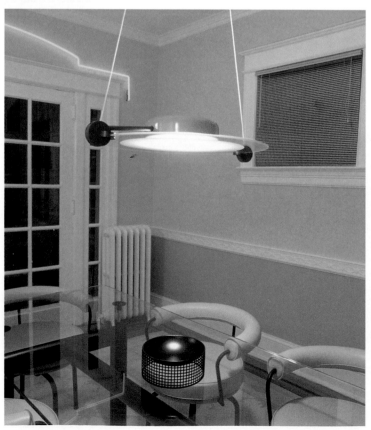

The silk dhurrie was selected especially for the room and brings the pale and peachy color scheme together.

Uplight from the glassblock cove in the headboard is illuminating the arched niche above the bed. The small niche containing the vase used to contain a shallow closet.

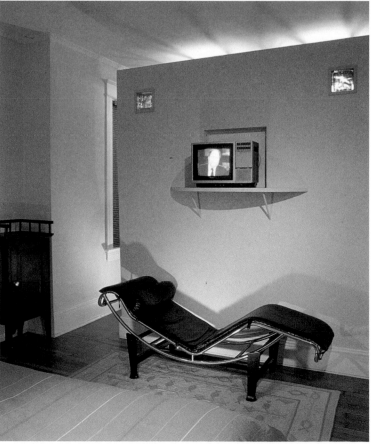

The freestanding wall at one side of the bedroom shields clothes from view. Fixtures located on the clothes side cast soft ambient light over the wall into the other half of the bedroom.

The master bath has been enlarged by combining two closets. A window has been added into what had been a solid wall, and a vent in the ceiling has been replaced by a skylight. The room is indirectly illuminated with uplight from bowl-shaped sconces.

The renovation took six months to complete, and cost $23,000, not including $11,000 for furnishings.

What had been a vent has been transformed into a skylight in the center of the bath. Other illumination includes wall sconces that uplight.

Unlike the other rooms in the house, which feature pastels, the bathroom, kitchen and studio are painted white and accented with black and primary colors.

Custom-designed "his" and "hers" wall cabinets hold toiletries so there is no need for counters and visible clutter.

The bulkhead above the bathtub holds speakers and a vent fan. There is a mirror mounted on the inside of the bathroom door for "her" convenience. The "his" cabinet has a car stereo, am/fm/cassette player mounted on the front base.

Chapter Three
One Room Wonders

Many lighting consultants are revamping their fee structures to include single day or single room/area consultations. This not only makes lighting design more accessible to those clients involved in partially renovating their homes, but to upper middle and middle class clients as well, who in years past could not afford to hire an interior designer, let alone a lighting consultant.

A guest's first impressions of a home can set the tone for the rest of the evening. Included here is an example of an entrance that has been transformed from an unimpressive split foyer into a gracious and spacious entryway that complements the rest of the house. Balance is the key in the architecture and in the lighting.

Perhaps the most popular candidates for renovation are the kitchen and bath areas. In this chapter, a condominium kitchen has been turned into an efficient, yet attractive room with the addition of a colorful neon sculpture, pendant fixtures, and under and over cabinet lighting. A perfect marriage of aesthetics and function.

A more elaborate white kitchen in a suburban home is fitted with a multi-use lighting system that makes the kitchen well-suited not only for day-to-day meal-making, but for evening entertaining. Black-painted theatrical track fixtures on a triangular truss system are in stark contrast to the sleek white laminate cabinets. Recessed downlights, and under and over cabinet fluorescents give the homeowner the option of using low-key lighting elements when entertaining is not a priority.

A dining room can be intimate and dramatic, and here we have an example of how carefully concealed PAR fixtures can precisely highlight art objects and architectural details without overwhelming the room. And a centrally located pendant provides a soft fill light at the table.

Since people are spending more time at home, the bedroom and bath have become centers of relaxation. The master suite featured has a whirlpool area equipped with mood-changing filtered fixtures that envelope the bathing area and its occupants in dark blue or pale rose light. Of course, the bath has ample additional illumination for grooming tasks. The bedroom's lighting system is carefully coordinated to echo architectural detailing.

A clear look at the difference lighting can make in a room is seen in the night and day versions of a white living room. By day, the room is almost uniformly flooded with daylight. But as the sun goes down, the lighting system allows the play of light and shadow to create interest and mood. Art objects and small scale furnishings are individually highlighted, and a glow from units placed just outside the windows to reveal exterior plantings makes the room a welcoming place to be. Quite a difference from what the room must have looked like originally with its single chandelier hanging from the center of the ceiling.

Landscape lighting is growing in popularity. Thoughtfully planned illumination makes the spa area shown here a little world of its own. Spotlighting the fountain and accenting the plantings surrounding the whirlpool visually expands the area, while maintaining its intimacy. Guests will feel they are in a garden and forget that the neighbor's garage is right behind the stone-clad facade.

FIBER OPTIC FANTASY

In the foyer, mirrored walls, and a fiber optic lit gold-leaf domed ceiling set the tone for what's to come in this Beverly Hills condominium.

What makes this condominium unusual from a lighting point of view is that it was one of the first extensive uses of fiber optics in an interior residential space. The condominium is located in a 26-story Beverly Hills complex. The design goal was to blend rich materials and sophisticated electronics to complement the entertaining lifestyle of the bachelor owner, and specifically to incorporate and showcase his collection of 1920s and 1930s authentic French show posters.

The entry foyer sets the tone for the apartment. It is marked by ceiling-height mirrored walls and a grey and white marble floor with emerald pickets. The gold-leaf ceiling is illuminated by fiber optics recessed into its perimeter. All the fiber optics units in the apartment use MR 16s and are looped to provide light that is uniform in intensity.

In the living room, the fiber optics are run just below the ceiling line around the perimeter of the room. Here the system is fitted with a rotating red/blue/green color wheel. The client can create an intimate atmosphere or enjoy an unobstructed view of the city via remote

PROJECT LOCATION
Beverly Hills, California
INTERIOR AND LIGHTING DESIGNER
James Blakeley, III, ASID, principal, and Tracy Utterback, project assistant, Blakeley-Bazeley, Ltd.
PHOTOGRAPHER
Chris Covey, Chris Covey Photographer
LIGHTING MANUFACTURERS
Capri Lighting, FIRE Ltd.

controlled metal blinds that disappear into the wall. Recessed MR 16s provide illumination in the interior of the room, and allow a nonglaring view outside.

The living room opens onto the dining area. Here another gold-leaf dome ceiling is lit around the perimeter with fiber optics. An incandescent chandelier is suspended from the center of the dome.

The kitchen has white lacquered cabinets, stainless steel backsplash and ventilation hood, black granite countertops, and a highly polished black granite tiled floor. The cabinets are "floated" with fiber optic lighting installed above and below them. Recessed incandescent fixtures provide general illumination in the center of the room, and a neon-banded clock above the eating area adds a touch of playfulness.

The conversation area furnishings in the living room include a ziggerat-shaped marble fireplace, lucite coffee table, and a baby grand piano. Stopped at one color for the photograph, the color wheel incorporated in the ceiling perimeter fiber optics system is normally in constant motion.

Above the lucite and glass table, and horn chairs is a chandelier and gold-leaf dome lit with fiber optics.

A playful touch to the kitchen is a neon-banded clock. Note the flexible spout in the eating area sink. It can be lowered and concealed beneath a custom wood chopping block. Water is turned on through the use of under-cabinet foot pedals marked "H" and "C".

The master bath is a study in black—black and gold marble countertop, black glass ceiling, black whirlpool tub, and an adjoining shower with one-way black glass. The lighting includes a horizontal strip of clear incandescent bulbs over the vanity, and waterproof fixtures installed in the whirlpool.

In the master bedroom, the curved platform on which the bed sits is echoed by the curved ceiling trough above. Fiber optics underlight the platform, and illuminate the perimeter of the gold-leaf ceiling trough. One MR 16 fixture highlights the French show poster above the bed. Wall sconces placed one either side of the poster provide ambient light and add visual interest.

In the kitchen, fiber optics are
installed both under and over
the cabinets. Appliances are
recessed into the backsplash.

Though not shown in this photo, fiber optics underlight the bed platform, and illuminate the perimeter of the gold-leaf ceiling trough.

Note the steamy underlit water in the whirlpool tub, and the television which drops out of the ceiling in the master bath.

Designer James Blakeley, ASID, notes that the apartment took over a year to complete because of all the electronics installed throughout it.

"For example, all the draperies disappear into the walls by remote control. There are three television sets that come out of the ceilings by remote control—one in the bathroom, one in the bedroom, and one in the media room/study. And in the media room, not only does the television drop down from the ceiling, but there is a projection television that also comes out of the ceiling with the screen," Blakeley says. "It was possible to do all these things because in these condos there is about 4 feet of space above the ceiling line."

CONTRAST AND CONCEALMENT

The pendant fixture uplights the redwood beam ceiling and casts a glow over the dining table.

The contrast of light and shadow in the dining area of this Portola Valley home is not photographer's fill light. It is the result of dramatic lighting design.

The dining room is marked by redwood beam construction.

"The apex beam is huge—24 inches deep, and about 10 inches wide," says lighting designer Randall Whitehead. "The way we did all the accent lighting was to mount low-voltage track fixtures on either side of this giant beam. The beam is so thick that the fixtures literally disappear into the dark where the roof meets the apex line."

The designer specified PAR 36 lamps because he needed a light source that would project a precise beam a great distance. The client wanted specific objects and areas highlighted dramatically, like the anemone on the mantelpiece.

"That beam is about 7 inches in diameter," says Whitehead, "and there isn't a type of MR 16 that could produce that tight a beam at that distance."

A drawback of PAR 36 lamps is that they "hum" when a standard dimmer is used. Whitehead was able to eliminate the noise on this project because he had the room available to install a variac dimmer.

PROJECT LOCATION
Portola Valley, California
LIGHTING DESIGNER
Randall Whitehead, Light Source
ARCHITECT
Spencer Associates
INTERIOR DESIGNER
Marlene Grant, Whitney Corporation
ELECTRICAL CONTRACTOR
Debcor
PHOTOGRAPHER
Mary E. Nichols
LIGHTING MANUFACTURERS
Lightolier Inc., Leviton Manufacturing Co. Inc.,
Hubbell Inc., Sylvan Designs, Inc., Phoenix Day

The client wanted light and
shadow contrasts, so precise
beams are used to dramatically
highlight mantelpiece objects
and the Japanese kimono.

"A standard dimmer is about the
size of a switch—4 inches by
2 inches," Whitehead explains. "A
variac dimmer is about 7 inches by
9 inches. It's been around since the
1940s, and the reason it works is
that it doesn't just reduce the voltage, but actually changes the voltage going to the fixtures, so there is
no hum. But you need a project with
enough space in which to install
these larger units."

To provide fill light in the space,
the pendant fixture over the dining
table is designed mainly to throw
light up. A diffusing lens prevents
much light from coming down.

"We just wanted to put a glow
over the table, with lots of light
going up without there being any
glare," Whitehead says. "We don't
normally do dining areas as dramatic
as this, but that's how the client
wanted the space to be, and you
have to listen to what the client
wants and needs."

Low-voltage fixtures also highlight
the kimono.

GRAND ENTRANCE

The exterior tile pattern is similar to that in the foyer. Two circular bulkhead, surface-mounted fixtures and three surface-mounted fixtures on the retaining walls illuminate the exterior.

After the addition of rooms at the back of this 4,000-plus square foot home in Alexandria, Virginia, the unrenovated entrance appeared too small and ungracious in comparison to the rest of the home. The entry hall was a "split foyer," so one climbed up steps outside the home, and entered it between the basement and living room levels.

"As you entered into this landing, the open door would literally eat up the entire foyer space, so you'd feel as if you were either going to fall on the stairs going down to the basement, or trip on the stairs going up to the living room," says Dhiru Thadani, whose firm was called in to transform the split foyer into a grander entrance.

The architect relandscaped the front yard and leveled it, so there was no need to step up to the front door.

"We built a foyer at the basement level and created a grand stair that leads up to the living room," Thadani says. "The trick about that stair is it's about 3 feet wide at the living room level at the top and 3 feet, 8 inches wide at the bottom basement level. It's the old Bernini trick that he used in the Scala Reggia at

PROJECT LOCATION
Alexandria, Virginia
ARCHITECT AND LIGHTING DESIGNER
Dhiru Thadani, AIA, and Peter Hetzel,
Thadani Hetzel Partnership
ETCHED GLASS FABRICATION
Ellen Kardell, The Kardell Studio
ENTRY DOOR, TRANSCOM AND
WINDOW FABRICATION
Harry L. Brittain, Culler Construction
PHOTOGRAPHER
Gordon Beall
LIGHTING MANUFACTURER
Conran's

Symmetry and balance distinguish the 12 foot x 12 foot foyer addition. Wood bands match door frame and window trims.

the Vatican to create an illusion of grandness. You think you're going to travel a long distance. In perspective, the eye converges the walls, but the staircase is physically converging as well, so the result is a kind of forced perspective.''

Behind the etched glass doors at the foot of the staircase is a coat closet on the left, and the basement recreation room on the right. At the top of the stairs, the living room is on the left, and the guest bedroom is behind the white wall on the right.

''We purposely made the room symmetrical and clean lined. It goes up about 20 feet and has a gabled ceiling,'' Thadani says.

''We feel strongly that a project is made with correct lighting. You can spend all this time on the form and the design and the architecture, but it doesn't look good if it is not lighted properly,'' Thadani says.

To continue the symmetry of the space, a pair of windows—the same type used throughout the house—was added into each side wall to create two very large windows in scale with the foyer.

''The upper window aligns with the house windows. It's high and it forces your eye up toward the trees and the sky outside, and not on the garage or the carport,'' Thadani says.

''To light the room to achieve a soaring feeling, we felt sconces would bounce light very evenly down off the gabled ceiling. We didn't want the owners to see the light source from the living room level, so the sconces are mounted 6 feet above the living room floor level.''

Why did Thadani use inexpensive metal sconces from Conran's?

''When you try to convince a client to use a lot of fixtures and say they are $300 apiece, sometimes you know it's not going to happen. But, for example, when you say, 'Let's use four fixtures at $160 total,' it's much easier to get the client to agree,'' Thadani explains.

Four wall sconces mounted at 15 feet above the finished floor —two on either sides of the windows— illuminate the gable ceiling of the entry foyer. Four surface mounted fixtures at 8 feet above the floor illuminate the lower section.

"These inexpensive metal fixtures always come a little warped. You can't put them on a wall that's flat. So as part of my spec on them, I require that, after they are mounted and screwed to the wall, the curve be caulked, so you don't get the light fill that comes down the sides of the fixtures and accentuates the warping."

A second fixture was placed beneath the sconces between two wood bands to light the foyer more evenly.

"The house sits up on a hill a good 30 feet above the street level, and it's become like a lighthouse beacon in the neighborhood," Thadani says.

On the exterior facade, round bulkhead fixtures are mounted on either side of the etched glass door. Three oval-shaped versions of those fixtures are installed on the railroad-tie retaining wall that wraps around and defines the 12 foot by 12 foot front tile patio.

The pattern for the etched glass door is derived from designs on the Chrysler Building elevator doors.

Four recessed downlights illuminate the staircase, which converges from 4 feet at the bottom to 3 feet, 6 inches at the top.

Here's one way to define high tech: combine sleek, white lacquered cabinets and granite tile flooring with black theatrical fixtures mounted on a finely webbed triangular truss system in a 900-square-foot remodeled kitchen in Livingston, New Jersey.

Lighting designer Corinne Strumpf, and her assistant, Elizabeth Gowrie, had to painstakingly measure each truss exactly so it could be angled and placed parallel to the next truss. And, all the trusses had to butt snugly up against the mirrored walls above the cabinetry.

The webbing has been left off the top of each truss to allow a row of outlets to be installed in the ceiling. The outlets, spaced 12 inches apart, accommodate tungsten halogen, black-painted adjustable fixtures that are mounted on the trusses. The theatrical-style halogen units can be moved anywhere along the runners, which are made larger than standard size to support their weight.

In between the trusses are recessed PAR lamps, three in each row. Additional task lighting is provided by fluorescent fixtures mounted under the cabinets. All the lighting, except the fluorescent fixtures, is controlled from a panel which allows for dimming and separate switching.

The mirrors on the walls above the cabinets, and on cabinet-free and appliance-free walls visually extend the trusses and make the kitchen seem even larger than it is.

The multiple options and adjustability of fixtures make the space versatile — comfortable for preparing a quick family meal, or for socializing with guests before a dinner party.

The versatile lighting system gives the homeowner a variety of options — under-cabinet task lighting, aimed truss mounted tungsten halogen fixtures, and recessed downlights.

PROJECT LOCATION
Livingston, New Jersey
LIGHTING DESIGNER
Corinne Strumpf, principal and
Elizabeth Gowrie, assistant, Corinne Strumpf
Lighting Design
INTERIOR DESIGNER
Reid James Dolson, Reid James Dolson
Interior Design
PHOTOGRAPHER
Darwin K. Davidson, Darwin K. Davidson Ltd.
LIGHTING MANUFACTURERS
Edison Price Lighting, Alkco, Lighting Services
Inc., Lightolier, all fixtures obtained through
City Lights

hough the view of Rock Creek Park from this 150-square-foot galley kitchen was spectacular, the appearance of the room itself was ho-hum—and this was after it had been converted when the building went "condo."

Dhiru Thadani was charged with breathing life and excitement into the space. He chose to divide the room into two zones: a work area, and an eating area.

"Both zones share a central axis," Thadani says. "A suspended light fixture spatially defines the eating area and reinforces the central axis. The sink and microwave form local centers on opposite walls of the work area and define a cross axis."

Dynamics in the space are created through juxtaposing two elements: color and line. A white backdrop is created with white laminate cabinets, wall panels, pantry doors and ceiling.

Color accents introduced both in lighting and surfacing elements play against this. A neon geometric pattern sculpture in yellow and blue fills a void above the sink. The ballast and transformer are concealed in the cabinet to the right of the sculpture.

Touches of royal blue—chosen to match the client's china—appear in floor tiles, cabinet handles, baseboard, recessed cornice trim, and the suspended light fixture. The backsplashes and countertops are a neutral gray/silver.

The clean vertical and horizontal lines of the laminate cabinets are reinforced by strict adherence to a 15-inch module for all doors, drawers, and wall panel widths. This works against the diagonal lines of the checkerboard floor pattern.

The transformer for the playful touch of neon is located in the cabinet on the right side.

PROJECT LOCATION
Washington, D.C.
ARCHITECT AND LIGHTING DESIGNER
Dhiru A. Thadani, AIA, and Peter Hetzel,
Thadani Hetzel Partnership, Architects
(construction management by architects)
CARPENTER
Louis Tenenbaum
ELECTRICAL CONTRACTOR
McCarty Electric Co.
PAINTING CONTRACTOR
Fred Jovel
PLUMBING CONTRACTOR
Blake & Wilcox
TILE INSTALLATION
Custom Design Tile
NEON
Marty King, Light'n Up Neon
LIGHTING FIXTURES
Illuminations, and Maurice Electric Co.
PHOTOGRAPHER
Gordon Beall

The suspended warm-white ceiling fixture in the work area casts 40 percent of the light up and 60 percent down. This provides soft, reflected ambient illumination. Task lighting on countertops comes from continuous under-cabinet fluorescent fixtures.

The pendant fixture over the breakfast table provides a decorative touch in the eating area. The unit's three horizontal glass planes allow minimal visual interference with the outside view. The fixture uses three 12-volt halogen lamps.

The remodeling was completed at a total cost of $25,000, including fees.

The thin, horizontal planes of the pendant fixture over the breakfast table allow occupants to enjoy a virtually unimpeded outside view.

Task lighting is provided by under-cabinet fluorescent fixtures, which have been placed evenly above the geometrically patterned neon.

The presence of multiple light sources allows the light levels to be changed to suit the occupants' mood and the time of day.

NIGHTTIME OASIS

What looks like a relatively open swim spa area by day is transformed into an intimate, private outdoor oasis by night through lighting designed by landscape architect Larry Tison.

"When you go there at night, you feel like you're in your own private little area," Tison says. "The swim spa is only about 18 feet from the house, and so there's a lot of light coming out from the interior entertainment/bar area to the swim pool," Tison says.

The swim spa is used to increase swimming strength. Motors push the water against the body and allow the occupant to go through the motions of swimming while remaining stationary. The spa also comes with a divider that can be inserted to separate it into cold and hot water sides. The hot water spa side is about 3 1/2 feet deep; the cold, plunge portion is about 5 feet deep. The interior of the spa is illuminated with one pool light recessed into one side of the spa.

Spotlights highlight a small rock fountain behind the spa, as well as selected surrounding trees and shrubbery. The low walls on either side of the pathway that lead to the spa are used for seating during parties, and are illuminated with low-voltage fixtures.

The swim spa is located in a relatively open space. The faux rock wall behind the spa is actually the neighbor's garage

PROJECT LOCATION
Burbank, California
LANDSCAPE ARCHITECT AND
LIGHTING DESIGNER
Larry Tison & Associates
PHOTOGRAPHER
Christopher Covey — Christopher Covey
Photography
LIGHTING MANUFACTURERS
Nightscaping — Loran Inc

"The back wall covered with rocks is the neighbor's garage. We received permission from them to add the rock facing. It's faux rock, actually. They look like round river rocks, but they are made of concrete and fiberglass," Tison says.

"The whole project was a design challenge because there is a limited amount of space in there," Tison says. "The precast swim spa had to be brought in with a 128 foot crane that was positioned in the front driveway. The crane had to swing the spa over the house to drop it into the backyard."

The master bedroom and bath suite designed for the owners of this Houston residence looks nothing like the rest of the house, which is marked by faux Georgian paneling and crown molding. Instead, architect Calvin Powitzky chose to give the suite a strong architectural feel via extensive use of soffits and wood banding.

Michael John Smith was called in to provide the lighting design for this Houston couple's home after the architectural design had been begun.

"There was no lighting in the space yet when I was called in— they really hadn't gotten to that point," says Smith. "The owner wasn't interested in using a bunch of decorative lamps, and when I saw the detailing of the wood bands around the ceiling, I jumped at the idea of perimeter lighting."

The suite consists of five areas: the foyer, bedroom, walk-in closet, dressing room, and bathroom. Horizontal wood bands that run at varied heights throughout the spaces visu-

ally unify them. Wall surfaces, coordinated along with furniture and fabrics by Grace Green, are mirrored, light oak or pale silk fabric.

The foyer contains a pair of circular wood columns and two cabinets. One cabinet is for storage; the other conceals the television.

Illuminating the artwork on the wall are recessed adjustable accent luminaires that use 12-volt PAR 36 wide floods. These fixtures are equipped with elements that are used in other units throughout the suite: gold Alzak trims in all the recessed fixtures to enhance the warmth of the spaces, and louvers to minimize brightness.

Small-aperture, recessed MR 16 downlights highlight art objects on top of the cabinets as well as the wood columns. The color delivered by the MR 16 fixtures has been altered by adding tempered, pale topaz glass filters to bring it in line with the warm ambience of the suite.

Reading light over the bed comes from 12-volt PAR 36 very narrow spot fixtures. Artwork is highlighted by 12-volt, 50-watt PAR 36 narrow spots.

PROJECT LOCATION
Houston, Texas
LIGHTING DESIGNER
Michael John Smith, AIA, IES, IALD
ARCHITECT
Calvin Powitsky, PBR Architects
INTERIOR DESIGNER
Grace Green, Greenfield Interiors
ELECTRICIAN
Rulon Electric
PHOTOGRAPHER
Frank Martin
LIGHTING MANUFACTURERS
Prescolite, Miniature Lighting Products:
Lightolier, Nova Industries, Norbert Belfer,
Illuminations "Phantom", Lutron Electronics
Co. Inc., Lite Touch

In the bedroom, the wood banding that runs along the perimeter of the room has been pulled away from the ceiling line by 3 inches. Installed behind the banding and separated by square metal baffles that minimize brightness and are painted to blend in with the oak paneling are 5-watt, 12-volt festoon lamps spaced at 5 inches on center.

The festoon lamps are used beneath the built-in bed platform to produce a "floating" effect and in the canopy above the bed for indirect illumination. The lamps are installed between metal baffles under the bedside shelving to prevent glare from reaching the bed.

Individually switched recessed adjustable, 12-volt PAR 36 very narrow spot fixtures provide reading light over the bed. Reading light near the chaise lounge comes from a floor lamp, which also provides fill light for the rest of the room.

Artwork above the bed is highlighted by two 12-volt, 50-watt PAR 36 narrow spots.

In the dressing room, sparkle and light for grooming comes from two rows of bare, 24-volt, 6-watt bayonet base lamps. One row is recessed into the oak band over the lavatory mirrors. The other is suspended in a brass tube over the mirrored closet doors.

The bedroom is distinguished by the wood band behind which 5-watt festoon lamps are concealed and separated by metal baffles.

The architectural detailing established in the bedroom is continued into the bathroom — via soffits and wood banding.

Additional task lighting at the countertop is furnished by louvered 12-volt, 50-watt PAR 36 recessed, adjustable narrow spots, and two 50-watt PAR 36 wide floods positioned to create a crowning glow for the person gazing into the mirror.

The architectural detailing of the bedroom is carried into the bath. But here, color filters add drama to the whirlpool area.

"I really don't use colored light very often. But I thought it would be fun and playful to use it here. The clients could make the bath as everyday or as dramatic as they wanted by changing the dimmers," says Smith. "Of course, I would never lock it in where they had to have the dramatic colors all the time—that would get old fast."

Dark blue, tempered glass filters have been installed in three 12-volt, 50-watt narrow spot, louvered fixtures. Pale rose tempered glass filters have been fitted to three additional narrow spot fixtures. Low-voltage dimmers control each color group and enable the user to produce subtle or strong changes in the mood of the space.

Groups of dimmers are controlled by miniature relay activating switches. The dimmers for the bedroom are installed in a concealed panel in the foyer. Those for the bath and dressing areas are in the closet.

Button panels with dimmer presets are located at the foyer entrance, at each side of the bed, and at each end of the dressing area. Preset scenes range from night light to full intensity.

Because current changes cause a dimmed lamp's filament to vibrate and produce a hum, filter chokes have been installed that reduce the sharp changes in current that occur from using dimming equipment. The chokes, because they also buzz, have been located remotely, along with the transformer, in a rain-tight box on the home's exterior. Lamp life is increased by using the dimmers and chokes, which slightly reduce line voltage.

Light from blue and rose color filters on 50-watt narrow spot fixtures blend to create a passionate purple in the bath.

Separate controls for each group of fixtures allow the clients to vary the mood and lighting intensity. Dimmers have been installed out of sight in the closet.

NIGHT AND DAY IN A WHITE ROOM

The pale fabrics and furnishings enrich the warmth of the sunlight that flows into and creates shadowplay in this living room during the day. At night, the interior designer wanted a more dramatic look without detracting from or overpowering the room's occupants.

Lighting designer Randall Whitehead devised an adjustable, ceiling recessed MR 16 system.

"We lit through the plants, so that you see shadow patterns coming down along the columns," says Whitehead. "We lit down onto the acrylic tables to make them 'float' in

the space and to highlight the objects placed on them. We have one light hitting the plate on the mantelpiece, and because the mirror is behind it, there's no spill light, so the plate seems to glow on its own.''

The fill light seen on the ceiling comes from two plaster wall sconces (unseen in the photographs because they are situated on either side of the photographer). The room's finishing touch is the glow just outside the windows to reveal portions of the plantings. This prevents the windows from seeming like black holes, or from acting like mirrors and reflecting what's in the room.

Before the lighting system was installed, the only fixture in the living room of this 1920s-built home had been a centrally placed chandelier. Though the power for the room was centered where the chandelier was, the design team was able to overcome this limitation with the help of the electrician.

"If the electrician had used a standard skill saw to cut the holes for the fixtures in the plaster ceiling, the plaster would have cracked and crumbled," Whitehead says. "Instead he used a hole saw—a sort of pie plate with teeth—to cut perfect holes up there. Then he used a right angle drill to make connections. So we were able to put in all those fixtures with no plastering or repainting.

See the dramatic difference lighting makes in the living room at night. An MR 16 system creates pools of light and dappled shadow patterns.

PROJECT LOCATION
Piedmont, California
LIGHTING DESIGNER
Randall Whitehead, Light Source
INTERIOR DESIGNER
Owner
ELECTRICAL CONTRACTOR
Electric Connection
PHOTOGRAPHER
Stephen Fridge
LIGHTING MANUFACTURERS
Halo Lighting, Hubbell Inc., Lutron Electronics Co. Inc.

FIT FOR A PHAROAH

Small wall washers softly highlight the Egyptian figures
painted on the wall. The
custom table contains an
uplight in the base.

The living room walls of this 1930s-built, Mediterranean-style home had been covered with black, grey and red wool plaid for approximately 18 years.

"And I don't know whether the walls moved over time, or if they were never done right, but they were not straight, and you know what that does when you add a plaid pattern," says interior designer Priscilla Schultz. Her assignment was to transform the cold and dingy room into a comfortable, livable environment when the owners lent their home out to be a showhouse.

Because the owners are Egyptian, Schultz chose to use Egyptian motifs throughout the room, and incorporated some of the owners' original art pieces.

"You have to be careful when a space is themed that it doesn't wind up looking like an amusement park," says Schultz. This is the only room in the home that is Egyptian themed, and that serves as an advantage. Guests are pleasantly surprised, as were showhouse visitors, when they walk down the staircase and are greeted by the open-armed Egyptian figure that has been painted on the wall at the base of the stairway.

The walls of the living room are adorned with more Egyptian figures, cement columns detailed with a faux stone finish, and details taken from the patterns of a typical Pharoah's headdress. The furnishings are in soft, neutral tones.

PROJECT LOCATION
Palos Verdes Estates, California
INTERIOR AND LIGHTING DESIGNER
Priscilla Schultz, Priscilla Schultz Interior Design
PHOTOGRAPHER
Christopher Covey, Christopher Covey
Photography
LIGHTING MANUFACTURERS
Nu-Tech Lighting, National Specialty Lighting
Company

Schultz reveals, however, that "If you take the lighting out of the room, it's a nice room, but it wouldn't have 'made it'."

Wooden blinds have been added to the full glass doorway on the left wall so the mood of the room could be controlled. In the center of the back wall is a custom-designed table containing a miniature reflector lamp that uplights its base.

The halogen wall washers high-lighting the Egyptian figures painted on the wall are small and unobtrusive — only 2 inches wide, and 2 3/8 inches deep. Though these are adjustable, the additional downlights installed around the perimeter of the ceiling are fixed.

To create a feeling of height in the just-under-8-foot ceiling, faux moldings that create the impression the ceiling is stepped have been painted on.

Both showhouse guests and the homeowners were delighted with the staircase handrail.

"It's made with acrylic, and it's ribbed, so you know that light is in there, but you can't see all the wiring and workings," says Schultz. "There had never been a railing there, but with the inspectors coming through to check the showhouse, there had to be one, otherwise there might have been a legal problem." As long as Shultz had to install the rail, she thought it might as well be something very special.

"I would say that three-quarters of the men who came through that room were enthralled with it, and a lot of the elderly ladies were as well, because it feels warm when you grab hold of it," says Schultz.

The rail contains low-voltage tube-lights and works with a transformer. Though it is available in different sizes, this particular rail is 8 feet long, supported with center and end posts.

The wall covering is actually painted pieces of paper torn in all different shapes and sizes. The muralist ran some of the paper from the wall to the ceiling, and painted the Egyptian figures over the parchment-like material so "it looks like it's been there since the beginning of time."

The wood flooring had not been in good shape, and the designer did not have the option of replacing it. So she had flooring experts bleach it

out, lighten it, and she had them add what looks like striping that mimics the lines in the headdress of one of the wall-painted Egyptian figures. The stripes were wiped off here and there, so they would look like they were worn.

The striped theme is seen also in the carpeting, which has a sewn-in white border, surrounded by a black leather edging.

Though this project began as a showhouse room, Schultz succeeded in attracting the owners' attention.

"The owners kept almost everything in the room," she says.

Chapter Four

New Products

New product development is driven by many factors, including the needs of the marketplace, the economic feasibility of producing a particular product, and breakthroughs in technology and research.

Concepts behind the trends in the development of today's lighting products that will continue to be refined in the future include: smaller, more compact light sources and fixtures; increased energy efficiency of sources and fixtures; improved color rendering of fluorescent and HID sources; increased ability to control and dim non-incandescent sources; the influence of European design in decorative fixtures; and the development of decorative fixtures that use other than incandescent sources.

How do these general developments relate to residential lighting specifically? Regarding light sources, the biggest surprise has been in the refinement of the compact fluorescent. I remember over a decade ago, there were efforts made by professionals and lighting companies to promote the use of energy-saving fluorescent fixtures in the home with little success. Back then, fixtures were bulky, and fluorescent came in only two flavors: cool white and warm white.

That's changed. Today, fluorescent is available in scores of sizes, shapes, and colors. The future will bring more fixtures designed specifically to house the compact fluorescent, so it will be viewed as a legitimate light source in itself, and not merely as a replacement in fixtures that previously used incandescent.

Compact fluorescent will probably begin appearing regularly first in work areas of the home—laundry rooms, kitchens, corridors, attics, basements, and home offices.

But the compact fluorescent isn't the only small-sized source that is being used more frequently in homes. Where PAR lamps used to reign as the most commonly used fixture type in homes with designed lighting, halogen and incandescent-based, low-voltage sources are beginning to predominate. The small sizes of these lamps and the fixtures designed for them are contributing to the increased appreciation of the delicate, small and refined look in light fixtures, and the increased awareness of effects of the light itself by the homeowner.

Portable and decorative fixtures are being made with more refined materials—handblown glass, treated metals, perforated and patterned metals, etched glass. The designs are sleeker, influenced by the growing number of European companies that are distributing their fixtures in the United States. More than ever, portable light fixtures are being designed and marketed as works of art in themselves.

Controls have increased in complexity. The standard in high-end homes is to include controls that offer a number of preset scenes, with manual overrides. In the future, the problem of achieving increased dimming and control capability for non-incandescent sources will be on the manufacturers' drawing boards.

Landscape lighting for aesthetic effect, as well as to provide safety and security, is becoming commonplace in high-end residences as well.

The popular technique of providing not just one kind of lighting, but varied types of lighting fixtures, and even sources, in a room—for example, ceiling-recessed, wall-mounted, and portable table fixtures—is a reflection of the homeowner's demand for increased flexibility, and bodes well for manufacturers of all lighting product types.

Though this chapter does not include all manufacturers of residential equipment, it is a wide-ranging sampling of what's available in the marketplace today.

Art Specialty Co.
Chicago, Illionis

The Citilamp line is a collection of lamps based on manufacturing specifications and Art Deco designs popular in the 1930s. Some of the lamps have been continually manufactured by Art Specialty since the 1930s. Others have been reissued. The model shown was originally designed to be placed on top of television sets in the early 1940s, when the public believed that watching television in the dark was harmful to the eyes. Citilamp finishes include metallic hues of silver, taupe-charcoal, rose, jade, and wrinkle black. Only metals are used in the assembly process—no plastic.

Hampstead Lighting and Accessories, Inc.
Irvine, California

The Germaquadro wall sconce from Italy was designed by Paolo Deganello and is manufactured by Venini. The sconce is made of white lacquered metal that forms an angular shape similar to a spiral. The six handmade glass rods that emanate from the housing are available in any combination of pink, blue, amethyst, yellow, green and red. The fixture houses two 100-watt halogen lamps.

Pass & Seymour/Legrand
Syracuse, New York

Impressions is a line of premium wiring devices and wall plates for residential and commercial applications. Models include wall plates with a smooth, screwless surface and interchangeable trim inserts that create dual-color plates. Sixteen color options are available in the wall plates. The line also features switches and receptacles, dimmers and ground fault circuit interrupters, transient voltage surge suppressors and telephone data connectors.

Tech Lighting, Inc.
Chicago, Illinois

The Nuvola floor lamp has a black and gray marble base with a frosted glass top. The bowl is supported by four metal rods that cradle a 'crystal ball' diffuser. The fixtures house a 300-watt T 3 halogen source and includes a dimmer.

Tech Lighting, Inc.
Chicago, Illinois

The Steel Feather wall sconce is designed for use in the Tech High-wire System. A diamond-shaped parchment diffuser is supported by a curved, perforated metal plate. The colored glass filter situated between the bulb and the diffuser gives off an eye-shaped glow.

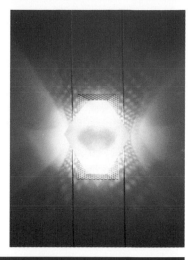

General Electric Company
Cleveland, Ohio

The MR 16 Precise with Constant Color coating is available in 20-, 35-, 50- and 75-watt versions. The constant color dichroic coating eliminates the discoloration of the reflector when viewed from the front, produces a white beam of light with no green or blue halos, and provides a more subdued blue light from the back of the lamp or fixture that is consistent from lamp to lamp over the life of the lamp. Rated at 4,000 hours average life,

the MR 16 Precise lamps with Constant Color coating will maintain more of its beam lumens throughout the life of the lamp and will not suffer gradual lumen depreciation due to a degraded reflector. The Constant Color coating will be on open-face and cover glass versions of the MR 16 Precise lamp.

Luxo Lamp
Port Chester, New York

The Luxo Halogen Task Lighting System is based on the Luxo articulated adjustable arm and is available in 25- and 40-inch sizes. The lamp head is directable a full 360 degrees. Models are available with translucent green or amber shades, or in opaque black for computer VDT use. The reflector maximizes output of a 35-watt, 12-volt halogen bulb. An in-line transformer has a quick-connect plug. Seven interchangeable base options are also available. The system is U.L. listed to safety requirements that went into effect in 1991.

DiBianco Lighting
Brooklyn, New York

The Elite pendant fixture has adjustable rod halogen suspension. The glazed blown glass diffuser is available in white, pink or blue. The frame is black lacquered metal. The length is approximately 30 inches by 10 inches. The minimum height is 35 inches; maximum, 51 inches. The maximum wattage is 300-watts halogen.

DiBianco Lighting
Brooklyn, New York

Nembo is a murano glass wall/ceiling fixture available in frosted white, green, rose, aqua or milky white glass. The length is 13 inches by 8 inches. The height/depth is 8 inches. The maximum wattage is 200-watts incandescent.

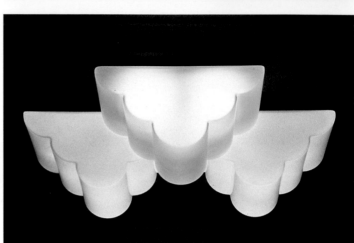

Winona Lighting
Winona, Minnesota

The Stripes wall sconce includes an acrylic half cylinder trimmed with three brass bands. Light is allowed to spill from the top and bottom through open ends. Fixture dimensions are 12 inches high by 6 inches wide by 4 inches (projection). The unit uses two PL 9 twin tubes, 120 volt. The Stripes sconce is part of the Cotillion Series.

Winona Lighting
Winona, Minnesota

The Zepher wall sconce is available with polished brass or chrome, and a black nextel paint finish. It is lamped with a 20 volt, 150-wall halogen mini-can. The unit measures 17.5 inches wide by 8.5 inches high by 8.0 inches projection. A complementary chandelier style is also available. The Zepher is one of six lighting fixtures in the Perf Light series. Each uses perforated metal as a central design element.

Joy Wulke Studio Of Art And Design
Stony Creek, Connecticut

Spangle is made of cracked glass panels framed in brushed stainless steel. The unit glints and glistens in daylilght, and glows in the evening. Joy Wulke has exhibited her sculpture and installation work in museums and galleries throughout the country and has worked with architects to produce commissions of exquisite beauty and sensitivity to the power of light to enliven form and space. Each piece is signed and numbered.

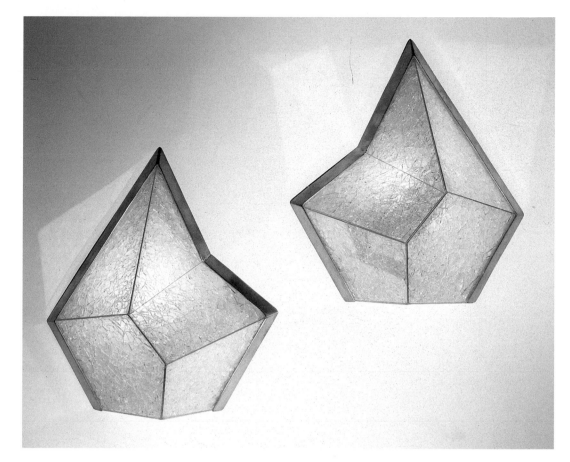

Conservation Technology, Ltd. (Con-Tech)
Deerfield, Illinois

This line of low-voltage recessed halogen fixtures includes multiplier, wall wash, eyeball, baffled and adjustable downlight designs. The units are U.L. listed, provide superior color rendition and house 20-, 35- and 50-watt halogen lamps. They are easily installed and aimed. A variety of trim colors is available.

Zelco Industries, Inc.
Mount Vernon, New York

Via Lattea is a milky way of 20-watt and 50-watt spot and flood lights suspended by a network of connectors and rods. Low-voltage halogen Stella heads, fully articulated, can be arranged to suit varied lighting requirements. The unit is easy to install without special tools. Via Lattea comes in three different carry-home kits, each with five or six lights, instructions and mounting components.

Baldinger Architectural Lighting Inc.
Astoria, New York

Max is a classic, square-shaped wall sconce that radiates direct uplight and soft indirect light from a 60-watt incandescent tubular lamp. The 12-inch square diffuser is offered in two options: white opal or clear frosted glass; or a unique perforated metal diffuser in white or black. Detail trim finished include polished brass, satin brass, white or black metal.

Baldinger Architectural Lighting Inc.
Astoria, New York

Ana is a rectangular-shaped wall sconce that radiates direct uplight and soft indirect light from a 60-watt incandescent tubular lap. The diffuser measures 12 inches high by 6 inches wide and is available in two options: white opal or clear frosted glass; or a perforated metal diffuser in white or black. Detail trim finishes include polished brass, satin brass, white or black metal.

Flos Incorporated
Huntington Station, New York

The Mira family of fixtures has been designed by Italian architect Ezio Didone, and consists of three designs. Each model measures 24 inches in diameter and radiates diffused downward lighting from a 200-wall halogen lamp. Each incorporates circular upper and lower diffusers that fit to a tapered aluminum body, creating a housing that when viewed from the side is saucer-shaped. The diffusers are made of pressed and etched glass with subtle patterning. The tapered body is available with a polished aluminum or a gloss black enamel finish. The Mira/S pendant shown is suspended from a black or chrome ''egg'' via three slightly curved chrome rods. The egg in turn is suspended from a black ceiling rose by a cord and three cables with a maximum length of 8 feet.

Flos Incorporated
Huntington Station, New York

Pierrot is a low-voltage halogen task designed by Afra and Tobia Scarpa. The fixture's arm and legs snap together and the lamp head can be snapped in, facing either upward or downward. Pierrot stands 17.6 inches high and has an overall length of 35.8 inches. Arm and legs are constructed of a composite material that enables current to be transmitted from the 50-watt toroidal transformer to the lamp head—no wires are needed. The base swivels while the arm, acting as a lever, can be placed in either an up or down position. Arm and legs are offered in blue-grey enamel with violet diffuser, turquoise with red diffuser, or natural copper with a clear coating and a green diffuser. The transformer base is black. The light source is 50-watt halogen.

GTE Products Corporation
Danvers, Massachusetts

This compact fluorescent lamp/ electronic ballas combination is rated at 18 watts and produces 1,100 lumens. The unit is designed to replace a 75-watt incandescent lamp and saves 57 watts of energy. Over its rated life of 10,000 hours, the Sylvania compact fluorescent lamp will save the end user $45.60 in electricity when replacing the 75-watt incandescent based on the national average power cost of 8 cents per kilowatt-hour.

Lutron Electronics Co.,
Coopersburg, Pennsylvania

The NeT*work Central Lighting Control System makes it possible to monitor and control lighting in as many as 15 lighted areas from one or more locations. The system links Lutron's Nova T Vareo dimmers, Nova T electronic touch switches, and Grafik Eye preset dimming controls with the NeT*work master control to create a central control system.

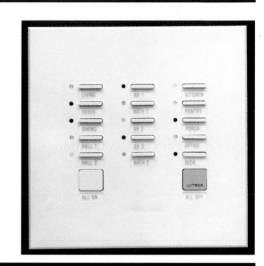

GTE Sylvania Lighting
Danvers, Massachusetts

Ths Sylvania subminiature fluorescent family consists of 20 lamps available in lengths of 4 to 20 inches, and in wattages of 1 to 13 with corresponding lumen ratings of 15 to 860. All have a diameter of 7 millimeters. The lamps are available in two color temperatures and have a triphosphor coating that provides a color rendering index of 80. The 3,000 Kelvin temperature is suited for task lighting and other applications requiring a warm color light. For lighting tasks where a cool, crisp look is desirable, such as backlighting, 5,000 Kelvin color temperature lamps are available. Lamps are available in hot or cold cathode versions.

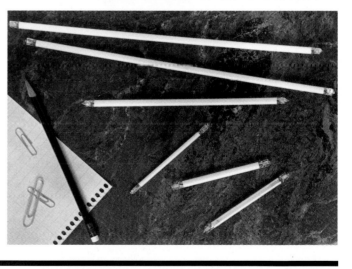

Capri Lighting
Los Angeles, California

An unusual undulating design is the theme for Wave LC220 trim, part of Capri's European Collection. The trim is available in four finishes, layered by hand application: sparkling gold, sable chrome, pearl white metallic, and a walnut effect that takes on the look of burl wood. The Wave LC220 accepts a variety of low-voltage lamps and offers a wide choice of wattages and beamspreads.

Pioneer Electronics Technology, Inc.
Pomona, California

The CSL series Garden Speakers combine a high-fidelity speaker and light in a sculptured freestanding acrylic polymer resin cabinet for wide variety of indoor and outdoor installations. Two models are available: the CSL-1000 in a rectangular (shown), and the CSL-2000 in a triangular enclosure. The two-way, air suspension, three-speaker system includes a woofer, two tweeters and has a maximum power handling of 150 watts. The Garden Speaker houses a built-in 12-volt light source. The sculpted enclosure looks and feels like natural marble or stone. The Garden Speakers are available in summer dusk, midnight granite and desert sandstone.

Matthew Lighting Studio, Inc.
Miami, Florida

The Glasgow Lighting Series is inspired by Scottish architect, Charles Rennie Mackintosh and is reminiscent of his work in geometric form. Shown are the tall wall sconce (TI 1202), and a small wall sconce (TI 1200). Available finishes are polished brass, satin black or white. The fixtures are illuminated by halogen lamps that are covered with acrylic diffusers resembling rice paper. The series also includes long, square and foyer ceiling fixtures, a medium-sized wall sconce, and a torchiere.

Juno Lighting, Inc.
Des Plaines, Illinois

The Strap Trac lights line includes both low-voltage and line-voltage units. The Line Voltage Series includes fixtures for 55-watt PAR 16, 50-75-watt PAR 30, and 150-watt PAR 38 lamps. The Low Voltage Series includes fixtures for 20-75-watt MR 16, and 50-watt PAR 36 lamps, and an adjustable round beam spot projector. Each Strap Trac light is available in short stem or integral pendant versions. Finishes include white, black, red and satin-brushed aluminum. Accessories include barn doors, beam controlling eyebrows, color filters, pattern lenses and louvers.

Gross Chandelier Company
St. Louis, Missouri

The World's Fair Collection of chandeliers and wall brackets features options such as suspended or flush mounts, white acrylic or faux alabaster translucent bowls, white opal or acid-etched glass shades, and polished or antique brass finishes. The World's Fair Collection is part of an entire series of new decorative lighting fixtures that includes the Sherwood, Protocol, and Masquerade Collections of chandeliers and coordinating wall brackets, and the Aristocrat Collection of wall brackets.

Con-Tech Lighting
Deerfield, Illinois 60015

Additions to the New Decade Series include four flat back and round back cylinder track lights with shortened housings to accommodate 120-volt PAR 20 and PAR 30 tungsten halogen lamps. A full baffle cutoff enhances accent light effects and helps reduce eye strain. Flat back models are stem mounted and round back units have yoke mount styling. Both insure 350 degree rotation. An on/off switch is provided and all are U.L. listed.

Reggiani USA
New Windsor, New York

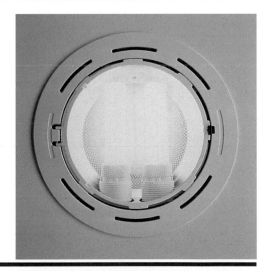

Techne downlights designed by Fabio Reggiani are available for use with compact fluorescent, high-intensity discharge, and line-voltage sources. The Techne downlights are designed to fit all popular ceiling systems, and are equipped with flow-through ventilation systems to provide excellent lamp life and reduced operating temperatures. The unit includes a protective glass closure that improves fixture utilization ratios and allows for easy cleaning.

Murray Feiss
Bronx, New York

Pendants from in-house designer June Hersh are from the Contemporary American Collection. On the left are Halophane and Railroad glass prism and brass pendants. On the right are custom-painted beige and white sand step aluminum models.

Hampstead Lighting And Accessories, Inc.
Irvine, California

Feltro is a suspension lamp designed by Cini Boeri and manufactured by Venini. The dish is made of opalescent glass. It is blown and hand-opened with a transparent thread on the edge. Supporting the dish are three adjustable steel wires that can adjust the height up to 56 inches. The dish is 22 inches in diameter and houses a 100-watt milk-white bulb. Feltro is available in opaline milk-white with a transparent aquamarine or green band, and in opaline pink with a red band.

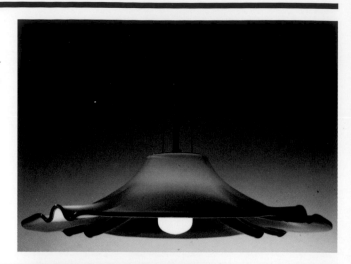

Leviton Manufacturing Co., Inc.
Little Neck, New York

The Decora line of lighting controls has been expanded with the addition of fluorescent dimmers. Rated at 120-volt 60 Hz, the dimmers are available in single-pole and three way, and can be ganged with incandescent and low-voltage incandescent dimmers, as well as switches and receptacles. The units feature a permanently mounted rocker switch, an integrated linear slide control, and a separate switch that allows for on/off switching without disturbing preset brightness levels.

Halo Lighting
Elk Grove Village, Illinois

The Deco Series are track fixtures that combine a traditional round back shape with two encircling lucite rings that transmit a soft, warm glow of light. The L1525 is 4 1/3 inches long and is offered in white, black, brass and black chrome. The two translucent rings measure 5 5/8 inches in diameter. The Deco lampholder can be used with a variety of light sources, including the 50-watt R 20 PAR 20 Capsylite or PAR 16 lamps.

Halo Lighting
Elk Grove Village, Illinois

Joining the Power-Trac line are two stylized lampholders with perforated shades. The L2700 model accommodates a 50-watt MR 16 lamp. The L2710 uses a 75-watt MR 16 lamp. The fixtures allow a limited amount of gentle spill light through the shades. The units, offered in white and matte black finishes, measure three inches in length, and are three inches wide, with a 6 1/8 inch extension.

George Kovacs Lighting, Inc.
New York, New York

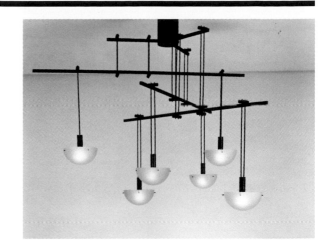

Suspenders fixtures, designed by Robert Sonneman, are based on delicate, spiderlike suspensions that form luminous sculptures of balance and aesthetic tension. The excitement of wireless low-voltage technology is created through a series of components—canopies, horizontal bars and vertical suspenders—which snap together and support elegant shades of frosted white or indigo glass. The model shown uses six 20-watt, 12-volt bi-pin halogen lamps. Glass shades are available in six styles and two colors.

Outwater Plastic Industries, Inc.
Wood Ridge, New Jersey

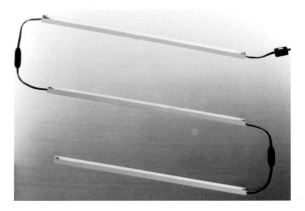

Connect-a-Light is an interconnecting lighting system that uses standard line voltage, and measures 1/2 inch by 1/2 inch. Polarized mating connectors with 18-inch wire leads allow connecting up to 150 lamps on a 30 10 inch lighting modules in any one run. The mating system powers entire runs with a single plug. Connect-a-Light includes 1.50-watt sub-miniature lamps, an on/off switch, and a polarized wall outlet plug with a 6-inch cord. Spacing is approximately 2 inches on center and may be changed to accommodate odd tube lengths. The product is available in polished brass, polished chrome, hi-tech black, and white, and in 10 , 20 , 30 , and 40 inch sizes.

Lightworks
Philadelphia, Pennsylvania

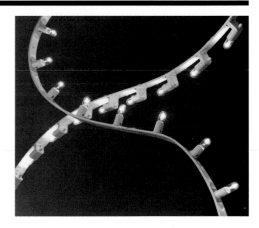

The RB Series RibbonLite is available with a halogen lamp option, vertical or horizontal sockets, six lamp wattages, several socket spacings from 1.2 to 12 inches, and operates on low-voltage. RibbonLite can be used for ambient lighting, downlighting countertops from beneath overhanging cabinets, and uplighting ceilings from cove niches. It can also be used to delineate architectural lines and outline buildings.

Koch + Lowy
Long Island City, New York

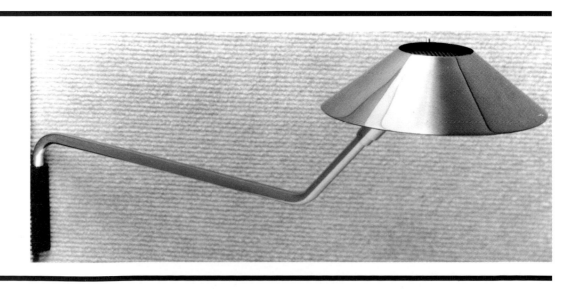

The STC Series includes incandescent, halogen and fluorescent models in a variety of styles ranging from classic contemporary to modern. These task lights attach to standard shelf uprights and most systems furniture. Shows is Ciao (STC-6).

Accessories International Inc.
Houston, Texas

The Chelsea Hanging Light, designed by Salman Shah, is equipped with a 300-watt halogen lamp and can be used with a maximum of 500 watts. The unit measures 46 inches wide and 42 inches high. Finishes offered are natural iron, verdigris, rust, sand, and antique gilt.

Juno Lighting, Inc.
Des Plaines, Illinois

The Cast 16 Series of track lights features a rectangular or cube-shaped format with rounded corners and integral miniature black baffles. The three models offered are: the T350 low-voltage rectangle with integral transformers; the T447 low-voltage cubed with electronic power pack transformer; and the T419 line-voltage cube utilizing a 55-watt PAR 16 lamp. Finishes are offered in black and white.

Nobert Belfer Lighting
Ocean, New Jersey

The Ramp provides shadowless, perimeter lighting. One compact fluorescent lamp overlaps the socket of the next to deliver 1,920 lumens per foot. The sockets are mounted on an extruded aluminum raceway.

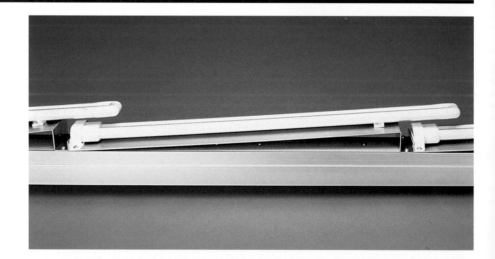

Litetouch Inc.
Salt Lake City, Utah

The Scenario is a stand alone, wall-mounted dimmer unit capable of controlling up to four dimming or switching loads with a total capacity of 2,400 watts. Each Scenario has four independent load control switches, four scene switches, and a master off switch. In addition, up to three remote nine-switch stations may be connected to each Scenario. The product is capable of connecting up to eight Scenarios to form an integrated system.

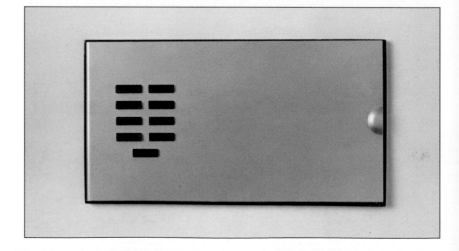

Brownlee Lighting
Orlando, Florida

The Madison-109 has a frosted glass diffuser surrounded by brass plated heavy gauge steel housing. The luminaire utilizes either one or two 13-watt compact fluorescent lamps. The unit measures 34 inches high, 15 3/4 inches wide, and 8 1/2 inches deep. A 277-volt ballast and/or an HPF ballast is available.

Lumenyte International Corporation
Costa Mesa, California

Starburst fiber optic is similar to tube lighting, but eliminates the maintenance problem of replacing burned out individual lamps. Points of evenly spaced light run along a length of Lumenyte Side Lighted Clear Coat optic. Spacing can vary based on the specific application, such as aisle, cover or glassblock lighting.

CSL Lighting Mfg. Inc.
Valencia, California

Multiples 948, designed by Sergio Orozco, contains over 948 style selections within one line. Stylistically related wall sconces, pendants, multi-pendants, chandeliers, and track fixtures are available. Glass and metal shades are interchangeable. The wide array of finishes includes black, white, polished brass, polished chrome, tortoise, verde, anthracite, and granite.

Norbert Belfer Lighting
Ocean, New Jersey

This linear directional display lighting fixture features low-voltage incandescent and halogen lamps on a continuous aluminum raceway. The two-way swivel socket combines with a wide selection of lamp wattages and beamspreads to offer maximum display lighting flexibility. The 2245 can be custom cut or mitre curved to shelf or cabinetry specification.

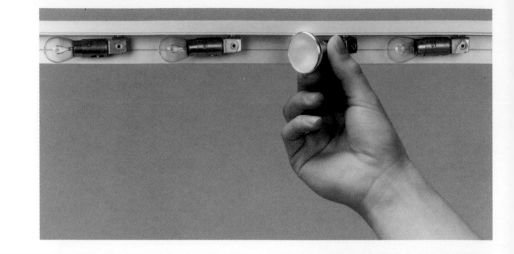

CSL Lighting Mfg. Inc.
Valencia, California

Tiny Track low-voltage track and track fixtures encompasses the Multiples 948 series of low-voltage halogen track fixtures, and is further augmented by PAR 36 and other MR 11 and MR 16 track fixtures. Tiny Track fixtures are only 3/4 inch wide and less than 1/2 deep. Shown is model 1443 in polished brass. Other finishes available for this model are black, white and polished chrome.

Illuminating Experiences
Highland Park, New Jersey

The Gran Rex Sconce, designed by Jorge Armando Garcia Garay, combines the richness of solid brass with clear glass accents. It measures 6 3/4 inches high by 14 1/2 inches wide with a 7 1/2 inch extension. The lamp uses a 300-watt 120-volt T3 Halogen bulb (included). Available finishes are solid brass or chrome.

Robert Long Lighting
Healdsburg, California

The Phoenix measures 6 inches overall height, 20 inches diameter, and 9 3/4 inches projection. It can be lamped with either incandescent or fluorescent, and is complemented by a related pendant fixture. Finishes offered are polished brass, chrome or copper, oil-rubbed bronze, or antique brass. Painted finishes are available on request.

Translite Systems
Redwood City, California

Translite Systems are low-voltage, safe bare conductor systems that use MR 16 lamps. Two power supply versions are offered: the portable model plugs into a grounded outlet and the permanent model is suitable for wiring in. Fixture selection ranges from minimalist fixtures to decorative pendants of Vianne glass from France, and Peacock fixtures in which each section of the fixture can be specified in a different color. Shown is the Micro Spot K with gold finish. It also comes in chrome, black and white finishes.

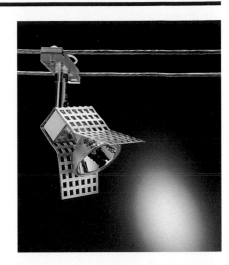

Philips Lighting
Somerset, New Jersey

Additions to the Masterline collection of halogen accent bulbs are PAR 20, PAR 30, and PAR 38 lamps. The PAR 20 and PAR 30 lamps can replace any R 30 lamp without an adaptor or socket extender. The long-neck design reduces the amount of light that is wasted inside recessed fixtures.

W.O.L.I.C. Inc.
Dallas, Texas

Starline is a flexible narrow width flat wire tapelight coated with insulating polyester PVC for indoor or outdoor application. The unit uses easily replaceable miniature lamps that are available in three spacings. It operates on a safe, 24-volt parallel circuitry that permits it to be field cut for a precise fit.

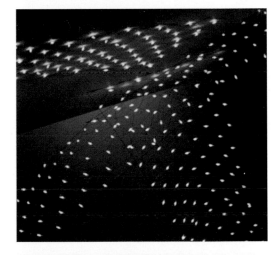

W.O.L.I.C. Inc.
Dallas, Texas

Jewel-Net is a grouping of 176 miniature long-life lamps connected into a heat resistant black wire cross-net of light for operation on 115-125-volt 60 Hz ac power. It is available in 24 inch by 86 inch size (maximum grouping of four nets on the same continuous electrical circuit/power plug) and is designed for use as a portable accent lighting product.

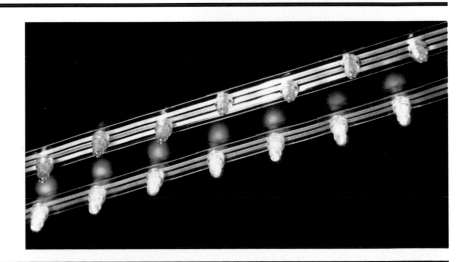

Chapter Five
Designers on Design

Who better to get an idea of where residential lighting has been and where it's going than from the professionals who design it. Included here are informal comments from the designers and architects who created the lighting systems for the projects in this book on the role of energy saving in residential lighting design, the acceptance and awareness of lighting design as a legitimate profession among residential clients, and what techniques in lighting might be increasing in popularity and use in the future.

Following is a summary of some of the key points. Though energy is the most important lighting issue of the 1990s, it will have much less of an effect on residential lighting than in the commercial sector. Though California's Title 24 does include stipulations currently for residences—the use of fluorescents in kitchens and baths—most states are far from mandating energy restrictions in residences.

Energy-conscious homeowners will probably begin replacing incandescent sources with more energy-efficient ones in work areas—like laundry rooms, corridors, and home offices. The high-end client, though seemingly willing to pay higher energy costs, and so more or less unconcerned with energy efficiency yet, is nonetheless taking a greater interest in maintenance.

Lighting designers do not see a swing toward more energy efficient sources as a hindrance to the effects their designs can achieve, mainly because advancements in product technology will probably keep up with the increased demand for more energy efficient sources. The past five years, for example, have seen the emergence of a plethora of fluorescent and compact fluorescent lamps in a wide range of sizes, shapes, and color temperatures. Lighting fixtures are getting smaller and this will eventually affect technique and design style in the future. Five years from now, there will be an even greater choice of product available than there is today.

Though many of today's residential clients are not aware, perhaps, that there is such a profession as lighting design, or exactly what it entails, they are more aware of light and lighting—like color differences among light sources, portable fixture design trends, and the relationship of flexible lighting to mood and ambience changes. One designer even feels strongly that the age of viewing lighting as a primary and tangible design element—and not just as a support element for architecture—is here.

In years past, when a design professional was hired to design a lighting system, the client expected the system to consist mainly of recessed architectural fixtures. Today, however, because of the greater variety of lighting fixtures and improvements in technology, the trend in technique is toward multi-layered systems involving combinations of recessed, track and decorative fixtures to provide flexibility in fulfilling task and comfort needs.

Future developments in residential lighting design probably will include greater interest in controls—so whole systems can be turned on and off at key locations—increased use of fiber optics, and landscape lighting, more use of lighting design services by upper middle and middle class clients, and more frequent inclusion of lighting professionals as a part of the design team at the initial conception stage of the project.

FRANCESCA BETTRIDGE
Cline Bettridge Bernstein Lighting Consultants
New York, New York

I think maintenance has become more of an issue, so that even clients in high-end residences are asking questions about the availability of the source, how long it lasts, what it's like to change the lamps, and how hard is it to use the fixtures. They are not always thinking anymore that they are going to have someone else, like a maintenance person, do it for them. They are thinking of themselves as the ones maintaining the lighting system.

Also clients are becoming more aware of the continuing developments in being able to control light and create paths of light. There is more of an interest in simplifying controls and not having a line of 10 dimmers. So there's more technical awareness and sophistication.

Clients are expressing light more in terms of color. They are more apt to say, 'I like warm light,' or 'I don't like that white light that's in a gallery'.

There seems to be more of an awareness out there that there are such things as lighting consultants. Ten years ago, the architect really had to sell the services of the lighting consultant, and who we were. But through education via magazines, books, newspapers, and word of mouth, people are more aware of the difference lighting can make. Today, people who don't understand anything about how lamps work or how fixtures work know that they went into a space and the lighting effect was spectacular.

There is also more of a tendency away from high contrast and dramatic pools of light. People don't really want to live like that in all black rooms anymore. They seem to want lighter colors and warmer colors.

There's more of a use of decorative fixtures. There are a lot more sconces being used, and combinations of sconces, pendants and torchieres, and less reliance on ceiling light.

RANDALL WHITEHEAD
Light Source
San Francisco, California

Our residential client base includes both upper and middle class clients. We often design one room at a time. Normally our charge is about $600—that is based on six hours of work per room or area—to lay out the lighting for a kitchen. So it's not as if you have to spend an enormous sum to hire a lighting consultant.

Regarding energy, here in California, we have Title 24 to deal with, which in residences requires that the ambient light in kitchens and baths of remodels of more than 50 percent or new construction be fluorescent. So we have had to reeducate people about the fear of fluorescent that we all had when we grew up, because all we had a choice of was cool white or warm white.

There are now over 200 colors available in fluorescent. Some are incredible, peachy, creamy colors that make people look wonderful. So we show clients how they can look, using the light boxes that are set up in most lighting showrooms. What's interesting is that most people will say they love incandescent light—the warm, amber glow. But they end up picking a color that's a fluorescent, because their hand placed in the light box looks so yellow and jaundiced under the incandescent light.

We find that it's a challenge to get fluorescent into some spaces without anybody knowing that it's fluorescent. We use indirect lighting above cabinets in the kitchen, or fixtures that look like domed skylights with fluorescent inside. And there are many things we can do now with the PL lamp.

STEFAN GRAF
Illuminart
Ypsilanti, Michigan

The first trend I'm finding is simply an awareness by the consumer that lighting is an important element. They are discovering the qualities of light, but very few are aware of the technology. They have some buzzwords that they throw around, like halogen, or low-voltage, or quartz lighting, but to them that could mean anything.

I think technology in lighting today is like audio technology was 20 years ago, in which the audio components first made their way to professional engineering groups who used them, but then the general public found out about things like graphic band equalizers, and developed a vocabulary for sound, and now everybody's an audio expert. I think the same thing is going to happen in lighting. People are going to become aware of these technologies and will start incorporating them into their homes.

I'm also finding that what's fundamental to us as professionals is very new to residential clients. For example, like low-brightness downlights are a whole new revelation. You say downlight to them and they imagine a black baffle unit with an R lamp exposed. So we have to go through a whole education process with our clients.

Lighting design is already becoming more widespread, beyond just wealthy clients. Small homeowners want help and we've set up a lighting clinic where they can buy an hour of our time. They have to bring an architect and their electrical contractor with them, and we give them advice and specifications, and let them do it on their own.

I think homeowners want things to be very basic and simple, especially when it comes to control systems. They just want to hit a switch and have everything work.

As far as technology trends go, I don't see much place for HID or metal halide in residential interiors, and I don't see a lot of recessed compact fluorescent units being popular in interiors residential work because being able to dim and control the atmosphere is essential. Even if energy gets very expensive, I don't find compact fluorescents something that will be used quite often, except maybe under counter cabinets, or for a task light here or there.

I see trends in the future toward the more widespread use of motion sensors. We like to specify motion sensors in the childrens' rooms, and even have the closet light switched on by opening the door.

Linear low-voltage lighting, fiber optics, motorized lighting technology developed originally for the theater and concerts, low-powered lasers, low-voltage MR 16 template projectors, and small discos or performing stages in basements and recreational areas are some of the fun things that offer clients the ability to change their lighting that may gain popularity in residences in the future.

DHIRU A. THADANI, AIA
PETER HETZEL, AIA
Thadani Hetzel Partnership
Washington, D.C.

Instead of citing a trend, we have a hope that people become more aware of lighting and how important it is in interior and exterior spaces. The mileage you can get out of even simple, inexpensive lighting is great. Our clients are becoming more and more convinced of that.

Regarding energy, as the technology changes, the light quality of fluorescent is getting better, and with higher frequency ballasts the lighting will be more efficient. Halogen lamps are more efficient. We relamp incandescent fixtures where we can with PLs. But it's the light quality that's important.

Dhiru Thadani comments, "I have this belief—it's my own individual notion of how to light a room—that you need multiple sources of light in every room. Do everything possible to reject the idea of one single light source at the center of the room—the single globe up there that every apartment building has. We try and talk people out of that.

But multiple sources of light can give you much more even lighting or create interesting shadows. If you have two fixtures equally placed around a window or doorway, they can create a scallop, of if the scalloping effect comes from a sconce the effect of the light can be art and a center in itself, and can reinforce the axis or the overall form of the room.

MICHAEL JOHN SMITH, AIA, IES, IALD
Michael John Smith Lighting Consultant
Houston, Texas

In the future, I think energy is going to be more of a consideration in residential lighting. But I hope we don't get into the mentality that plagued the country after the energy crisis a decade ago. It took ten years before people started putting Christmas lights up again.

I also think fiber optics will be playing a role in residential lighting. I just finished doing a sculpture that used a system of glass fibers. It's incredible how much light comes out from a 20-watt, MR 16 when it's spread around through fiber optics. I think the idea of having just a few sources in a building that will transmit the light to specific areas will become popular in the future. The spaces would be cooler and have less effect on air-conditioning because the heat from the light source can be contained in another area.

The average homeowner will become more aware of lighting, because they will be concerned about energy costs. Right now, I know too many people who are getting rid of the incandescent bulbs in their reading lamps and putting in PL lamps.

I can't imagine using them that way in my home. But I think that children who grow up with PL lamps in their homes may be comfortable with that in their adolescence and old age. That PL source in the table lamp will feel homey to them. It will never feel that way to me.

The new white SON, high-pressure sodium source has a beautiful color and a very long life, and is more efficient than quartz. We may start seeing that in more interior spaces, and perhaps for indirect lighting in residential areas, but used very judiciously, and with great care for the color of the wall or ceiling that the lighting is bounced off.

CRAIG ROEDER
Craig A. Roeder Associates
Dallas, Texas

We seem to be getting more residential projects these days. They are also more difficult to design than commercial projects because you're dealing with personalities and a degree of intimacy with the client. Designing the owner's vanity can be a nightmare, for example. It's not like you can solve the problem with something that all clients will like, because they all want something different.

Most of the clients who hire a lighting designer want something kind of glamorous. It doesn't mean we do glamorous kitchens, because kitchens include areas where you need to work. But even in a kitchen, we might use A-lamp downlights or include a neon cove, and then put in a few low-voltage accent lights, so late at night they can dim it down to a pretty little setting.

Regarding the energy situation, I think the good thing is that the manufacturers are coming up with some really acceptable alternative light fixtures. For example, the 2800 degree Kelvin PL lamp in the right fixture is a wonderful solution.

The key even to the type of lighting we do, which tends to be a little more glamorous, is to go ahead and use some energy where you need it. Do it in the lobby of a hotel, and then use some neon in the meeting rooms. So when we work on a major project, we try to balance out the energy in the building. If I have one area that's 10 watts per square foot, I'll have another that's 0.8 watts per square foot.

We're using more and more neon, which we are finding is very energy efficient. And it can last 10 years. I have installations we completed five years ago that still operate without a problem.

In a residence, where we used to specify an A-lamp cove, now we're doing 2800 degree Kelvin neon. The effect is identical to an incandescent cove and the neon dims beautifully. When you have an A-lamp cove, you're using 25 watts every 6 inches, but a neon cove is 9 watts per square foot—that's a big difference. Of course, you have to have a very sophisticated neon contractor install it.

PAMELA HULL WILSON
Pamela Hull Wilson Lighting Consultant
Dallas, Texas

I think that today, hiring a lighting consultant to design lighting
in residences is much more popular. Clients are more sophisticated, and see that the whole package of interior design includes lighting, and the creation of a more
dramatic night scene.

Regarding energy, I don't feel it affects higher-end clients at all. At the
same time, I don't think there are as
many large extravagant homes being built in Dallas as there were
10 years ago. However, those clients
that are building are interested in
lighting design, when 10 years ago
they hadn't heard of it.

CHIP ISRAEL
Grenald Associates Ltd.
Culver City, California

Here in the state of California we have Title 24, which says that in bathrooms and in kitchens you shall use fluorescent lighting. To us, that's not a great shock, because we are familiar with fluorescent lamps, and we know what a good high-color rendering lamp can do. But it's a large educational process trying to convince owners that fluorescents are their friends, and that they should be using them, and that they don't have to use cool white lamps that turn everything grey or green that they had been accustomed to in the past.

Obviously, the clients that we get involved with know what a lighting designer is. They usually have large scale, custom homes. But recently, we have been doing more and more spec houses built by developers who know they are going to sell a house and make a big profit on it. They don't want to go to the complexity in a lighting system that you see in the custom homes we have done, but they want something better than one light in the middle of the room.

Probably the biggest trend in residential lighting that's coming up is the automation of the lighting systems, whether it's wallbox controls, or a computer to run the entire house. And these systems work well from both a security standpoint — if you hear a noise, you touch one button and all the lights come on — and from a convenience standpoint — when you go to bed you can turn all the lights off in the house from one location without running from room to room.

Probably the biggest problem that's occurring now is that people are hearing about how great low-voltage MR 16s are, and they want to use them anywhere and everywhere. They can misapply a very good light source, and create a very harsh or improper lighting solution.

JULIA REZEK
Grenald Associates Ltd.
Culver City, California

Among strictly custom home-owners, energy will not be as much an issue as in the condominium market, and also the hotel market, which is considered residential/hospitality. In those other areas, compact PLs, for example, will be used widely in table lamps and retrofit type fixtures in the future. But the high-end residential custom homeowners are not ready to make that transition—they can afford their high energy bills.

And there's nothing in legislation coming up for Title 24 in California that is going to require homeowners to limit themselves energywise, except in kitchens and bathrooms. So in kitchens and bathrooms in custom homes, we'll be seeing the use of more fluorescent, because the West Coast inspectors are cracking down now.

Regarding the use of architectural lighting, and decorative or freestanding fixtures in residences, I see a developing trend toward the use of both. There are many interior designers who are trying to integrate the two, because when only recessed downlighting is used, sometimes you can wind up with a kind of harsh environment. I think many interior designers, and lighting consultants as well, bring in freestanding fixtures just to supplement that and give it more of an intimate residential feel.

I am an advocate of using freestanding and decorative fixtures, because I have a background in decorative fixtures, and I see that there is a need to integrate both into the home. I know that in the 50s and 60s, it was the popular trend to have only architecturally integrated lighting, but I see a trend toward the use of more decorative fixtures these days.

Regarding awareness of lighting, clients are not necessarily more aware of architectural lighting designers, but they are more aware of the type of lighting designers that produce good looking fixtures. A trickle-down effect has occurred because of stores like the Pottery Barn, that reach the consumer. The widespread availability of the high-tech or Italian look lighting fixtures that even the average person is being exposed to is making people more aware of lighting in general.

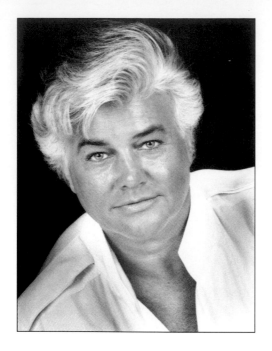

JAMES CALLAHAN, IALD
James Callahan Design Corporation
Palm Springs, California

I take energy conservation into consideration in my designs, but we have energy codes in California that say that every house has to have flourescent lighting in certain areas. And if you try to put something unusual in those areas, you won't get a permit to inhabit the residence.

If anything, I'm concerned about heat. The new bulbs—like tungsten halogen—put out a tremendous amount of heat, which puts a tremendous amount of pressure on air conditioning and cooling resources. I think the answer is not to discriminate against people who are willing to pay for the burden of energy consumption, but to work on conserving energy in more practical applications —parking lots, baseball fields, underground shopping centers, or even retailing.

But to inhibit a client in their residence from having an emotional experience through lighting designed by a lighting designer is actually interfering with my ability to explore, to learn and to earn a living. I think the answer is to give clients what they need, and what the job requires, as opposed to just what codes say or necessarily just to use what's available in your particular area.

Now, I had eight years experience as a therapist prior to my design career. One of the most fascinating parts about what I think I do as a designer is to envision myself in my client's shoes. If I accept what I see in them as a reflection of what they're all about and I dig a little bit deeper, I find that inside every one of my clients is this 'somebody' that's trying to get out—a private self that perhaps never got to grow.

As a designer, I get to tap into this, and my client is amused, excited, enthused and motivated to go further, because what we've really done through design is to revitalize that subdued personality.

We jokingly talk about the nouveau riche, but the fact is in this world, all money is new today. And we're a very young country—we can hardly compare ourselves with the Sistine Chapel people. But the fact is that, designwise, Europeans shed all their roccoco and their gilt, and have come out with perhaps the most forward thinking designs in automobiles, furniture, and fashion. It's ironic that Americans still try to hang on to what we thought we were, instead of what we came here to establish in the first place, as our own identity.

We seem to keep recapitulating the past. All that is important to us seems to be on a traditional level, as opposed to a futuristic level. Perhaps it is because the future's so ambiguous, or we have so little confidence in it that we go back to what's proven successful. But even the Europeans didn't do that. That's always bothered me and it's something I fight for with my clients.

CORINNE STRUMPF, IALD
Corinne Strumpf Lighting Design
Ringewood, New Jersey

I n California, energy is an issue for residential lighting, but it has not been addressed so far in the eastern part of the country. Though an energy-efficient source like compact fluorescent, for example, can be used successfully for work spaces in kitchens, laundry rooms, and for lower level recreation rooms, there are limitations. For one thing, you lose a lot of flexibility, because right now dimming compact fluorescent sources is prohibitively expensive on a residential scale. And in high-end homes with 20-foot ceilings, the compact fluorescents don't work well, because they don't project light far enough.

For living spaces, there's a quality of warmth and contrast achieved between incandescent lighting, which is dimmable and flexible, and low-voltage or halogen accent lighting that would be too great a loss not to have it in a residential space.

I think lighting design is becoming an accessible art to clients other than the wealthy. For instance, I do one-day wonders for people who are middle class. When the house is under construction, we'll go in, look at the blueprints, and give the owners notes on what to use and where to use it. We'll give them as much information on a design that we can pack into a day, and leave them to execute it. So that brings fees for a lighting consultant down from thousands to a few hundred dollars. This approach has a lot to do with how much responsibility the homeowner is willing to take on.

Design is reaching the mass market in other ways as well. Many types of high-end residential products are being knocked off by the mass market lighting manufacturers. Some of the decorative fixtures that came out of designer houses ten years ago are now showing up in $39.00 versions in Conran's. It's taken a long time for it to filter down, but it has filtered.

JAMES BLAKELEY
Blakeley Bazeley Ltd.
Beverly Hills, California

Clients are wanting more and more dramatic looks, like grazing columns, soffits, under furniture lighting, and floating tabletops. They are looking for something that separates their house from the Jones' house. Now that all the houses being built are cookie-cutted out, clients are trying to do something with the lighting in their houses to make theirs a little different than other people's homes.

LARRY TISON
Larry Tison & Associates
Burbank, California

People seem more interested in lighting today than they did ten years ago. In almost every project we do now, people make that part of the package and request lighting design. Whereas five or ten years ago, I would suggest it and they would say, 'Gee, we hadn't thought about that.'

And what I tell my clients basically is that there are three types of outdoor lighting. There's security lighting—the 'flood everything' concept where you put a couple of floodlights up in the corners of the building. And those are fine for when you're not home—they can be connected to a timer.

And then there's functional lighting which lights up the space you're going to use in an aesthetically pleasing manner. Finally there's background lighting, which gives depth to the landscape—for example, by highlighting a tree, a piece of sculpture, a waterfall or fountain. Explaining the purposes of lighting in those terms enables clients to grasp the concept very easily.

TULLY AND KALYNN WEISS
Tully Weiss Lighting Design
Dallas, Texas

The lighting business has changed significantly in the past decade. We've been in business for almost 13 years now, and in the very beginning, on the calls that we'd make to architects, we'd introduce ourselves as lighting designers. The majority of the professionals we spoke to thought of lighting designers as theatrical lighting consultants. At least, here in Dallas.

Now, on almost every important project, the architect will bring in a lighting consultant.

In the product area, I've noticed a lot of European thinking has been adapted in lighting equipment. When the small projector lamps were first introduced, and the PAR 36s came out, a lot of U.S. manufacturers had huge fixtures to house these little lamps. But suddenly, we're beginning to see smaller lighting units.

Client awareness has increased. Five or six years ago, when the MR 16 was being introduced, if you told a client that you were going to use a 2200 Kelvin lamp, or a 3000 Kelvin lamp, they wouldn't know what you were talking about. But now many clients are aware of the color temperatures of quartz halogen light sources. People relate sodium or metal halide to a color, especially in retail, whereas ten years ago if you asked a prospective client if they knew the difference between a high-pressure sodium and a metal halide lamp, they would not have known what you were talking about.

I think energy codes will affect what lighting designers do for a while. But we're seeing higher quality fluorescent downlights, and smaller metal halide equipment being introduced now, so in two to three years, we're going to see a bigger change that will enable the lighting designer to use HID and the fluorescents and still be creative with playful patterns of light.

PRISCILLA SCHULTZ
Priscilla Schultz Interiors
Palos Verdes Estates, California

Clients are more aware of lighting than ever before. For example, the people passing through the showhouse (included in this book), for example, are interested in low-voltage and halogen. And I'm surprised at the number of people who know there are such things. You think that these people just go to the store and buy a bulb, but that isn't true.

You would think that most of the men, who are brought to see the showhouse by their wives, wouldn't care about the interiors but the questions they ask are most interesting. They wanted details on the lighting handrail, and on the ceiling illumination.

MIGUEL RODRIGO-MAZURE
Rodrigo-Mazure Architects
Maimi, Florida

I think the industry has many kinds of halogen lamps—in narrow and open beams, and many fixtures that give you the opportunity to provide different lighting effects. We tried to create a theatrical effect in the "Glass House" project by using different sized beams to create different moods.

In the last 10 years, there have been so many more possibilities for creating varied effects because of the new types of equipment available. We're always on the lookout for new, more sophisticated hardware. We were the first ones in Florida, for example, to use the new Ada track light from Lightolier.

ROBERT ROSS
Robert Ross Incorporated
Culver City, California

Clients are willing to accept light as an element of contemporary design in the same way they accept wall finishes or pieces of steel or wood or shapes in architecture. Lighting has become almost one of the primary elements of design, as opposed to what it was before—an element to support the architecture. I design a lot of projects with light as the source of the design, and then I make the architecture conform to that. I'll want to pull out a wall and get light behind it, so that concept dictates what I have to do with the architecture, as opposed to the other way around.

Today, clients are willing to accept light as an 'object' in design because much of the lighting that's produced today, both decorative and architectural, is so wonderful. In years past, lighting was a sort of mystery—somehow you turned the light on and you were restricted to the bulb. Now, lighting is a flexible tool, because of the availability of such a wide range of bulbs and lamps, and what they have done with them—whether they are exposed just as bulbs, or hidden beautifully in wonderful architectural and decorative fixtures.

When you look at the way light has been used traditionally, it's essentially been used architecturally—you'd think, 'I'll have a downlight' or 'I'll have wall sconces'. But now it's being used as something that can shape color and pattern on the wall, something that can bring recessive and far away walls very close to the fact that the light can be focused and dealt with very precisely. The technology doesn't rely on the bulb anymore in the way it used to. You can use light as an escort to take you through a space, or you can use it to read a book.

I also find a lot more intimacy in lighting because of the range of dimming flexibility and the size of the bulb photometrics. You can use a lot of layers and points of light, and not just have light coming from one source. You can take the 150-watt bulb you might have used as a downlight years ago and split that up in terms of 10 locations which would give you the same lumen output, but also a sense of being able to control, manipulate, and play with the environment.

It's not just task and ambient lighting anymore. Light is an element of comfort, and comfort currently in our culture is a factor in what home is all about.

Instead of lighting being some ethereal element which no one understands, it's almost like the lighting is water and you can see it.

Once you understand the concept that lighting is a real element that you perceive and feel energetically, it becomes real on the level of its creating your relationship with your immediate environment.

Unless you are super wealthy, you're going to be living in some space which has to rely on lighting in order for you to manipulate it or change it, or give it interest or diversification.

INDEX

LIGHTING DESIGNERS

Blakeley III, James (Blakeley-Bazeley, Ltd.) **173, 232**

Booziotis, Bill (Booziotis & Company) **28**

Burke, Eileen **86**

Callahan, James (James Callahan - A Design Corporation) **9, 37, 230**

Cline Bettridge Bernstein Lighting Design **78, 111, 115, 147, 219**

Graff, Stephen (Illuminart) **150, 221**

Grenald, Ray (Grenald Associates) **20, 55**

Hetzel, Peter (Thadani Hetzel Partnership) **63, 86, 165, 181, 187, 222**

Israel, Chip (Grenald Associates) **46, 48, 227**

Marko, Alan **86**

Ng, Catherine (Light Source) **59**

Rezek, Julia (Grenald Associates) **20, 55, 228**

Robert Ross Inc. **120, 237**

Rodrigo-Mazure, Miguel (Rodrigo-Mazure Architects) **49, 236**

Roeder, Craig A. (Craig A. Roeder Associates Inc.) **71, 91, 127, 224**

Schultz, Priscilla (Priscilla Schultz Interior Design) **200, 235**

Smith, Michael John **192, 223**

Strumpf, Corinne (Corinne Strumpf Lighting Design) **24, 184, 231**

Thadani, Dhiru (Thadani Hetzel Partnership, Architects) **63, 86, 168, 181, 186, 222**

Tison, Larry (Larry Tison & Associates) **43, 190, 233**

Weiss, Kalynn (Tully Weiss Lighting Design) **104, 234**

Weiss, Tully (Tully Weiss Lighting Design) **28, 104, 234**

Whitehead, Randall (Light Source) **59, 81, 83, 99, 179, 197, 220**

Wilson, Pamela Hull (Pamela Hull Wilson, Lighting Consultant) **142, 226**

PHOTOGRAPHERS

Aaron, Peter (ESTO) **115**

Beall, Gordon **63, 165, 181, 187**

Brooke, Stephen **78**

Choi, William **147**

Cook, Robert Ames **71, 91, 127**

Covey, Christopher (Christopher Covey Photography) **43, 173, 190**

Davidson, Darwin K. (Darwin K. Davidson Ltd.) **184**

Delbeck, Thomas **47**

Freeman, Tina (Decatur Studio) **111**

Fridge, Stephen **83, 197**

Hursley, R. Greg (R. Greg Hursley Incorporated) **28**

Irion, Christopher **81**

Israel, Chip (Grenald Associates) **46**

Janken, Ben (Janken Photography) **59, 99**

Korab, Balthazar **150**

Lettich, Sheldon **9, 37**

Martin, Frank **192**

Miller, Robb **20**

Mills, William **165**

Nichols, Mary E. **179**

Pruitt, Richard **104**

Ritter, Frank **24**

Smith, Michael John **192**

Thadani, Dhiru A. **86**

Weschler, Thomas **150**

Wilson, James F. **104, 142**

Yoshimi, Toshi **55**

Lighting Manufacturers

Accessories International Incorporated **214**

Alesco **28, 127**

Alkco **99, 184**

American Neon **120**

Amerlux **55**

Art Specialty Company **204**

Artemide Inc. **63, 104, 143**

Artigraphics **55**

Baldinger Architectural Lighting Inc. **208**

Bega **55**

Broesche **81**

Brownioo Lighting **215**

Capri Lighting **9, 20, 37, 55, 78, 111, 115, 120, 150, 173, 209**

City Lights **184**

Cline Bettridge Bernstein Lighting Design **147**

Conran's **63, 165, 181**

Conservation Technology, Ltd. (Con-Tech) **207, 210**

CSL Lighting Manufacturer Incorporated **215, 216**

Devine Design **49**

Devon **150**

DiBianco Lighting **206**

Edison Price **24, 71, 78, 104, 111, 115, 127, 147, 184**

Electro Controls **24**

Express Light Ltd. **55**

Fire Ltd. **173**

Flo3 Incorporated **208**

GE Lighting **150**

General Electric Company **9, 205**

George Kovacs Lighting Incorporated **213**

Gray Glass Company **150**

Gross Chandelier Company **210**

GTE Products Corporation **209**

GTE Sylvania Lighting **209**

Halo Lighting **55, 59, 99, 197, 212**

Hampstead Lighting and Accessories, Inc. **204, 212**

Harry Gitlin Lighting **78, 115**

Hubbell Inc. **142, 179, 197**

Hydrel **71, 127**

Illuminating Experiences **216**

Illuminations "Phantom" **192**

Ingo Maurer **104**

Joy Wulke Studio of Art and Design **207**

Juno Lighting, Inc. **210, 214**

Keene Lighting **55**

Koch & Lowy **213**

Kurt Vcrsen **71, 150**

Lazin Lighting Inc. **104, 142**

Lee **150**

Leviton **63, 86, 179, 212**

Lighting Services Inc. **104, 184**

Lightolier Inc. **24, 28, 46, 59, 71, 78, 81, 83, 86, 115, 147, 179, 184, 192**

Lightworks **213**

L'Image **59**

Lite Cycle **28, 104**

Litelab **91, 127, 150**

LiteTouch **150, 192, 214**

Lithonia **150**

Loran Inc. **20, 99**

LSI Lighting Systems **142**

Lucifer Lighting Company **28, 81, 120**

Lumenyte **215**

Lumiline **9, 20, 28, 55, 63, 78, 81, 83, 86, 91, 99, 111, 115, 120, 127, 150, 192, 197**

Lutron Electronics Company **20, 28, 55, 63, 81, 83, 86, 91, 99, 120, 192, 197, 199**

Luxo Lamp **205, 209**

Matthew Lighting Studio Ltd. **210**

Miniature Lighting Products **104, 192**

Moldcast **55**

Murray Feiss **210**

Nagouchi and Hubell Inc. **59**

National Specialty Lighting Company **200**

Nightscape **43**

Nightscaping-Loran, Inc. **190**

Norbert Belfer **24, 71, 78, 127, 147, 192, 216**

Nova Industries **9, 192**

Nu-Tech Lighting **200**

Osram Corp. **91, 142, 150**

Outwater Plastics Inc. **213**

Pass & Seymour/Legrand **204**

Philips Lighting **217**

Phoenix Day **83, 179**

Pioneer Lighting Technology **210**

Prescolite **46, 49, 192**

Prudential Lighting **55**

Reggiani **55, 210**

Robert Long Lighting **216**

Ron Rezek **55**

Ron Wommack **10**

Roxter **9**

Sentinel Lighting Company **120, 147**

Special FX **150**

Staff Lighting **37**

Stonco Lighting **142**

Strand Controls **71, 127**

Sylvan Designs Inc. **120, 127, 179**

Tech Lighting, Inc. **204, 205**

Tivoli **150**

Translite Systems **217**

Tully Weiss, IPI **104**

Winona Lighting **206**

W.O.L.I.C. Inc. **217**

Zelco Industries, Inc. **207**